Sensational Memory

– CHRIS HARE –

An environmentally friendly book printed and bound in England by
www.printondemand-worldwide.com

This book is made entirely of chain-of-custody materials

Chris Hare

www.fast-print.net/store.php

Sensational Memory
Copyright © Chris Hare 2011

All rights reserved

No part of this book may be reproduced in any form by photocopying or any electronic or mechanical means, including information storage or retrieval systems, without permission in writing from both the copyright owner and the publisher of the book.

All characters are fictional.
Any similarity to any actual person is purely coincidental.

ISBN 978-178035-208-4

First published 2011 by
FASTPRINT PUBLISHING
Peterborough, England.

Chris Hare

Chapter 1

If you have the mental ability to read this paragraph, count to ten and visualise (not memorise but simply visualise) each of these following things: Train, Milk, Chimpanzee, Stamps, Snake, Forest, Tank, Clown, Trumpet and Flame - then you have the capacity to develop a Sensational Memory!

The aim of this book is to help you quickly achieve a better use of your memory. Just by reading the first few pages you will have more of an understanding of how your memory works. You will soon be able to prove to yourself that you have an amazing capacity for memory.

Most people feel they have a poor memory because they lack confidence in their mental agility. By using this book your confidence will soon grow and you will be able to apply your newly acquired skill in many everyday situations. This book will give you the tools to justify this newfound confidence. It will not be long before you are amazed at the outstanding results that you will accomplish.

This book will not just benefit people who feel they have a hopeless memory. It will also benefit people who believe they have a naturally good memory. Whatever your standpoint, it is my intention that after reading this book you will reach the dizzy heights of excellence.

By reading this book you will acquire the skill of remembering names and faces. You will learn how to remember important dates such as birthdays and anniversaries. You will also learn how to quickly memorise passages of text for examinations and speeches.

Surprisingly, if you are able to remember just 10 letters you will be able to remember and recall 99 different things. We are going to memorise a list of items numbered from 1 through to 99. By using a simple technique you will soon be able to recall any one of the items at random. For example, if you were given a random number such as 67 you would be able to recall immediately the corresponding item. You would also be able to give the corresponding number to any of the items listed.

It will become quickly apparent how this system works. However, although I will positively encourage you to create your own mnemonic images, it is important to study the dynamics of each and every example that I have outlaid for you in this book.

Throughout the course of this book I will give you useful information and techniques on how to improve your memory in general. By learning and applying these techniques you will find that your natural memory will improve.

This first effective memory technique works by translating numbers into letters so that we can create images that we can visualise in our mind.

What you are about to learn is called the Mnemonic Alphabet. Do not be afraid of this word "mnemonic". A mnemonic is simply any memory aid such as tying a knot in a handkerchief or writing something down.

The 10 letters that we are about to learn are T N M R L S F K P Z.

Let's deal with the first three numbers and letters first.

Number 1 is translated into the letter T simply because the letter T has one vertical stroke.

Number 2 is translated into the letter N simply because it has two vertical strokes.

Number 3 is translated into the letter M simply because it has three vertical strokes.

Now let's create images to represent the first three numbers.

1. The letter T.

We need to find a word or noun that is for some reason associated with the number ONE. For example, if the first thing you do in the morning is have a cup of tea then use a TEA bag as your mnemonic image.

Or if you play golf you will know that the first thing a golfer does is TEE-off. So you could use an image of a TEE peg.

2. The letter N.

Let's think about a word beginning with the letter N that we can associate with the number TWO. In this instance we can picture Noah from the Old Testament. Noah was the man who built the Ark where the animals entered TWO by TWO.

It is better to use an image of the Ark as opposed to an image of an old man. This is because when we see the Ark we know that we are referring to something that is associated with the number two. If we just had an image of an old man we might not so easily make an association with the number two.

3. The letter M.

In this instance we borrow the everyday phrase of "M for MOTHER". You can choose either an image of your own mother, of a pregnant woman or preferably an image of a woman pushing a pram.

A pram is a better image because we can imagine movement and placing things inside a pram.

Now let's see how we can implement the mnemonic words and images for enhancing our memory. We are now going to remember and recall three different objects or articles.

1. Slug

2. Apples

3. Wheelbarrow

For remembering that number 1 on our list is slug we imagine we are making a cup of tea and when we remove the TEA bag there is a slimy slug lying on the steaming TEA bag.

Alternatively, if you were to use the golf imagery you can imagine a golfer going to place his TEE-peg in the ground but

Sensational Memory

the TEE-peg is stabbed through a slug, which in turn spills its blood and guts. If we use violent and repulsive images we will be able to recall them with ease.

For remembering that number 2 on our list is apples imagine that there are hundreds of apples rolling down the gangplank of the Ark whilst the animals are going in TWO by TWO. Picture the animals trampling and squashing the apples and their hooves slipping as they try to walk the gangplank. Make sure that you can see the colours of the apples.

For remembering that number 3 on our list is wheelbarrow we picture a woman pushing a pram with a wheelbarrow on top of it. But picture the wheelbarrow wobbling, toppling and almost falling off. If we use a sense of danger in our images this will reinforce our image.

Let's now look at the next four numbers, letters and images.

Number 4 is translated into the letter R, but the image is DOOR. Use the image of a DOOR because it rhymes with FOUR. We use the letter R because it is the FOURTH letter of the word dooR

Let's say that a NURSE is the fourth thing on our list. We simply picture a nurse in her uniform pushing a syringe into our imaginary DOOR. However, it is advisable to use an image of a DOOR that is already familiar to you. Your memory works well when you attach new information to an old and established memory.

Number 5 is translated into the letter L. The mnemonic word is LAW but because LAW is a concept that we can't immediately image we have to find an image that represents LAW. A

POLICEMAN is a representative of the LAW that can easily be imaged.

Imagine that we can see our POLICEMAN holding his hand as if to stop the traffic. The image of a hand with its four fingers and a thumb can easily be associated with the number FIVE. Furthermore, if we imagine the hand with the thumb at a right angle we will have an L-shaped image (L for LAW).

Let's say the fifth item on our list is a STEAM IRON. Picture a steam iron being pressed into the palm of the POLICEMAN's hand. Feel the pain, see and hear steam from the iron and also see the brown scorch mark in the shape of an iron on the POLICEMAN's white glove. If the image of the brown scorch mark on the glove seems comical to you so much the better. Humour is another powerful tool that should be implemented wherever possible to reinforce our images.

Number 6 is translated into the letter S. We use the letter S because the sound of the number SIX sounds like a hissing sound. However, we can allow ourselves some alternatives but similar sounds, which we can use to our advantage. Words that begin with SH and CH can also be used to represent the number SIX. So let's take the letters SH and use the word SHOE to represent SIX. To reinforce our association with SIX and SHOE, imagine a SHOE with three lace holes each side totalling SIX. The pattern of the lace holes with a little imagination could appear like the six dots on a die/dice.

Let's make NETTLES the sixth item on the list. Imagine you are walking through a field of nettles whilst wearing a tight fitting pair of SHOES. As you walk through the nettles you can imagine that you are stung on the inside of your foot. It is so painful that you have to push your finger inside the SHOE to ease the pain. Picture the GREEN nettle leaf between your finger and foot inside your SHOE. Colour is another important tool to implement wherever possible.

Number 7 is translated into the letter K. To understand why we use the letter K takes a little imagination. If we look at the letter K and ignore the vertical stem of the character we can imagine that there is an inverted SEVEN to the right of the stem.

Now let's create a mnemonic image using the sound of the letter K. In this instance we will use the word COW. Although the word COW is spelt with the letter C, it is a hard sounding C that sounds similar to a K. Using this system the correct spelling of words is not important. It is the phonetic sounds that we are interested in because it is these sounds that inform us what number we are remembering. In this example we can spell the word COW with the letter K (KOW). A misspelt word is usually quickly drawn to our attention. We can use this to our advantage, as in this example (KOW).

Let's take the word HOLIDAY as the seventh item on our list. The word holiday can conjure up several images. Let's use a few representational images in our image.

Imagine a COW (KOW) sat in a deckchair on a beach with a bucket and spade wearing a knotted handkerchief and sunglasses.

Number 8 is translated into the letter F. Here again we need to use a little imagination. Sometimes we see the letter F written in a figure of eight shape (f).

However, in our next example we are not going to use the letter F, we are going to use an image of a PLATE because it rhymes with EIGHT. But because we are using the letter F in future examples I want you to imagine a stall of PLATES at the fair or fête (fête rhymes with PLATE and EIGHT).

Let's say the boy's name ANDREW is the eighth item on our list. Picture the pattern on a PLATE as the flag of Scotland (St ANDREW the patron saint of Scotland). This flag is easily recognisable with its dark blue background and white diagonal cross.

Number 9 translates into the letter P. This is simply because the letter P looks like an inverted number 9. The mnemonic image for NINE is PEA (green garden PEA). We can also use the letter b for the same reason. We could also have an image of a BEE (with its very distinctive black and amber colours). In addition we use the word LINE because it rhymes with the number NINE.

Let's say the ninth item on our list is a SLICED LOAF. So let's imagine that we take NINE slices of loaf, place them in a LINE and place a PEA on each slice (or BEE on every slice).

Number 10 is translated into the letters T and Z. Use the letter T for the same reason as in our first example (one vertical stoke in the letter T). We use the letter Z for ZERO to represent the figure 0.

Using the sounds of the letter T and Z we need to find a word that we can associate with the number 10. In this instance we can use the word TOES (as in TEN TOES). Remember we are only interested in the phonetic sounds and not the correct spelling.

Let's say the tenth item on our list is the French word *fromage*. In this example, we are going to stretch our imagination. If we think about children's clothes they often have a small label inside stating FROM AGE (FROM AGE 7-8 years or 9-10 years etc.). Let's imagine we have something irritating the gap between our TOES. When we remove our sock and shoe we discover one of these labels stuck between our TOES. Again we can use our sense of humour to help retain the image. The French word *fromage* means cheese and as we are thinking about TOES we can think about smelly cheesy feet. So for a few moments picture the label between the TOES and imagine the smell of cheesy feet.

We have now learnt the 10 letters T N M R L S K F P Z of the Mnemonic Alphabet.

Exercise 1

By following a simple procedure we should be able to recall each of those ten items at random. Let's do a short exercise to prove the effectiveness of the system. Take 10 small pieces of paper and number each one from 1 to 10 and place them in a paper bag. Randomly select one of these numbers. Translate the number to its corresponding letter and then recall the mnemonic image that we have created using that letter. Go through the whys and wherefores of how we created that image. Repeat the exercise until you have removed each number from the bag. With a little practice this process will involuntarily also bring up an image of that item from the list.

Try to do this exercise mentally without referring to the above text. Repeat the exercise 3 times so that you become familiar with the process and the 10 letters of the Mnemonic Alphabet.

Chapter 2

We are now going to look at how to memorise and recall items numbered 11 through to 19. We have already established that number 1 is translated to the letter T. Consequently, all the mnemonic words from 10 to 19 will start with the letter T.

Before creating the mnemonic image using more than one of the mnemonic letters, let's look at some important guidelines for using the Mnemonic Alphabet.

Try to make the words as short as possible. Usually this can be achieved by placing just one or two vowels between the mnemonic letters.

Here is a simple mnemonic sentence to help create mnemonic words, "Use VOWELS, HOW & WHY" between mnemonic letters to create mnemonic words. Notice that vowels (AEIOU) and the letters in HOW & WHY are not one of the ten Mnemonic Alphabet letters (TNMRLSKFPZ).

Number 11 is translated into the letters T and T. Here we make a word up simply by placing the vowel O in between the two mnemonic letters to create the word TOT. Although we can create other words by placing a vowel in between, the word TOT is probably the most effective. We can easily imagine a TOT picking something up and throwing it or screaming and reacting.

Let's say the eleventh item on our list is a dictionary. Picture a TOT with a dictionary tearing and throwing the pages. If in real life you were to go home and find a TOT really ripping the pages from a dictionary you would not forget this incident in a hurry. Any violent or shocking incident that stirs our emotions is easily recalled by our memory.

Ensure that you specifically see a dictionary as opposed to any other type of printed material.

Number 12 is translated into the letters T and N. Again by simply placing a vowel in between the two mnemonic letters we can make several words, but TIN is probably the most effective. This is because objects can be placed in a TIN; a TIN can be rattled to make a sound. It can be rolled (for example down a hill) thus giving us action or movement. A TIN can also be dented creating a violent or shocking act.

Let's say the twelfth item on our list is a mobile phone. Imagine a mobile phone is placed inside a TIN and when the phone rings its rattles the TIN. See the TIN as a shiny metal TIN. The fact that it is shiny makes it more prominent in our image.

In this example we can look for other associations to help reinforce our mnemonic. Most of us at some time have made a very simple telephone by using two tins joined together over some distance with a piece of string. Here we can make the association with communication, i.e. a TIN and a mobile phone. Although it is not always possible to make such associations with any two given objects, it is worthwhile to take advantage of any such opportunities should they arise.

Number 13 is translated into the letters T and M. The mnemonic word can be TOMB. You can allow yourself some licence and picture a gravestone with a cross. Here we can find some connotations to cement using the word TOMB to represent the number 13. Thirteen has connotations with the word TOMB because it is considered a number of ill fate. The 13th card of a tarot deck is the death card. Here we are drawing upon commonly existing information to our advantage.

Let's say the thirteenth item on our list is wasps. Simply picture wasps crawling over the cross of a TOMB. In fact, we can use an image of a cross to represent 13 as it is a simple and commonplace image.

Number 14 is translated into the letters T and R. Here we may place the two mnemonic letters together and make the word TREE. Remember that when we are creating mnemonic words it is preferable to keep the mnemonic letters as closely together as possible because our minds will be searching for the phonetic sounds to recall the information that we require. Ironically, students of mnemonics, when first learning, often struggle to find the mnemonic word for number 14 because they try to search for a word that has other letters between the mnemonic letters T and R. Of course, with the mnemonic word TREE the two mnemonic letters are standing side by side.

TREE is an excellent mnemonic image to use. A TREE has shape, form, movement, colour and it is easy to imagine attaching objects from its branches or trunk. Also, as discussed, the mnemonic letters are the first two letters of the word.

When creating mnemonic images try to avoid using words like tear (rip), or tear (cry) Although they may be simple words to create, they are not that easy to visualise or as versatile as a TREE.

If you were to use tear (rip) you might picture a tear in someone's clothes. However, your mind would focus more on the colour and style of clothes than the word tear. Also, it is preferable to use a word with a rolling R, as in rabbit as opposed to hare, to represent the number 4. It is this rolling R sound that is more emphatic and will signify the number 4 more easily.

So let's take our image of a TREE to represent number 14. Let's say the fourteenth item on our list is scissors. So picture several pairs of scissors hanging from the branches of the TREE. See the scissors as silver scissors that glitter and shine. Our minds quickly detect things that glitter and shine.

In this example we have another opportunity to find an extra association with the mnemonic image and the object that we are going to remember. The associated word in this example is the word 'cut' because trees are often cut and scissors are implements for cutting. So let's make an alternative image. Imagine a bizarre image of a giant pair of scissors cutting down a TREE.

Another powerful tool to use in memorising is exaggeration. For example, imagine the scissors being as large or even larger than the TREE that is being cut down.

Do not be afraid to make your images seem bizarre or ridiculous; as mentioned previously, humour is a powerful tool at our disposal.

The number 15 is translated into the letters T and L. The mnemonic word can be TAIL. I suggest that you picture a tiger's TAIL as it has the same distinctive black and amber colours as mentioned in our example of number 9 with the image of a BEE. In nature, black and amber often signifies danger. Wherever possible, make use of natural phenomena to stimulate your senses, albeit imaginary. As mentioned previously, the risk of danger is a very strong agent for stimulating mental energy.

Let's say the next item on our list is a table. Simply imagine a tiger's TAIL wrapped around a table. However, it is advisable to picture a table that you own or are familiar with. We have already touched upon how memory works by placing new information with old and established information.

I am sure you can easily imagine your surprise if you were to visit a foreign country with a completely different culture and yet if you were to see an exact replica of a table that you owned it would send a jolt of energy through your metabolism.

To expand upon our image for item number 15, we can use another powerful tool, which in this case will be the tool of substitution. Instead of simply wrapping a tiger's TAIL around a table, substitute the table legs for tigers' TAILS. Imagine the table walking about using the TAILS as moving legs.

The number 16 is translated into the letters T and SH. However, you may recall that the number 6 can be represented by the letters S, SH, CH (there are several alternative mnemonic letters for other numbers which help us create mnemonic words). For now let's concentrate on the number 16 using the letter T and SH.

The mnemonic image is TASH as in the abbreviation for the word moustache (tache). Let's say the next item on our list is an orange. Simply picture a man with a thick, bushy TASH/moustache (exaggeration) sucking an orange with the pips and juice dribbling over the hairs of the TASH (repulsion).

We can also use another technique called blending. This is where we match the colour of the mnemonic image with the article that we are trying to remember. In the above example we can make the TASH a ginger/red haired colour, which almost matches the colour orange. Let's reinforce the image even further. Imagine that the man's lips are made of orange peel (bizarre). Here again we find some more associations. A moustache can be associated with mouth, mouth can be associated with lips (rhymes with pips), oranges can be eaten, and eating is associated with biting and the use of a mouth. When you have this image of a man with a TASH sucking an orange, also imagine the sound of a man sucking a juicy orange (sound). Although in this example we have created a lot of associations, it will take only a spilt second of reflection of your image to find these associations. More often than not only one association is sufficient and, with a little practice, you will quickly and naturally find such fitting associations.

Number 17 is translated into the letters T and K. The mnemonic image that uses the letters T and K is TICK TOCK, but we will in fact use the image of a CLOCK. Let's say the seventeenth item on our list is rhubarb. Here again we are going to use the tool of substitution and replace the hands of our clock with sticks of rhubarb. Picture the colour and texture of the sticks of rhubarb.

To reinforce our association with the number 17 have one stick of rhubarb pointing to the number 12 and another shorter stick of rhubarb pointing to number 5. This time can be expressed as 17.00 hours (5pm). You will also notice that 12 and 5 add up to make 17.

Number 18 is translated into the letters T and F. The mnemonic image that uses the letters T and F is the word TOFFEE (although the word toffee has a double F we are only interested in the phonetic sound of one syllable to represent any given number).

TOFFEE is a good substance to use because it has various properties such as stickiness and taste and is also malleable. Let's say our eighteenth item on the list is a gorilla. Imagine a gorilla beating his chest, but as he beats his chest imagine that there are long sticky strands of TOFFEE which are debilitating his movement.

We can also picture strands of TOFFEE in between the gorilla's top and bottom set of teeth. We can imagine further still the gorilla with mixed emotions of being restricted by the stickiness of the TOFFEE and yet enjoying the sweet taste of the TOFFEE.

The number 19 is translated into the letters T and P. For this we can use an image of a TEE PEE or a WIGWAM but it would be too tense (2 tents)! I make no apology for the joke because I cannot emphasis the use of humour enough. However, in keeping with using the mnemonic letters forming one word let's use the letters T and P and use the image TAP. Let's say the nineteenth item on the list is an alarm clock. Imagine that you are asleep in bed and you are woken up by the sound of an alarm clock. Imagine that you are able to reach out and turn on a TAP that drowns the sound of the alarm.

Exercise 2

Take some more pieces of paper and number each one from 11 to 19. Add to the other pieces you made in the previous exercise numbered from 1 to 10. Randomly select one of these numbers. Translate the number to its corresponding letter or letters and then recall the mnemonic image that we have created using the letter or letters. Go through the whys and wherefores of how we created that image. Repeat the exercise until you have removed each number from the bag.

Remember that the process is in three parts:

1 Translate the numbers into mnemonic letters.

2. Recall the word or image created by those letters.

3. Finally recall the item on the list that is attached to the mnemonic image.

Again, try to do this exercise mentally without referring to the above text. Repeat the exercise twice so that you become familiar with the process and the images you have created.

Exercise 3

I'm now going to give you a very challenging exercise. I'm going to ask you to memorise and recall these digits in sequence: 14235763920613966278461127752143391853

But wait! Don't panic! I'm going help you. You may recall the opening paragraph of this book:

If you have the mental ability to read this paragraph, count to ten and visualise (not memorise but simply visualise) each of these following things: Train, Milk, Chimpanzee, Stamps, Snake, Forest, Tank, Clown, Trumpet and Flame - then you have the capacity to develop a Sensational Memory!

Take a closer look at the 10 things listed in the paragraph. Pick out the Mnemonic Alphabet letters from each of those words. You will soon see a pattern emerging that matches the 37-digit number I have asked you to memorise:

Train (142) Milk (357) Chimpanzee (63920) Stamps (61396) Snake (627) Forest (8461) Tank (127) Clown (752) Trumpet (14391) Flame (853)

The human mind functions very well when it is following a story. That's why millions of TV viewers will sit and watch soap operas, plays and films. The human mind likes to be kept curious and likes to follow a sequence of events.

In a moment we are going to create a story using the things from the list. But another important thing to remember is that the human mind likes to quantify things. It asks questions like: How far is it? How long does it take? How many are there?

We are going to number the ten sequences using a different system from the Mnemonic Alphabet. This is so that we do not get confused with the images we have used learning the items we have learnt from 1 through to 19.

I have already mentioned that we learn new information by attaching it to established information. Most of us have learnt a sequence of numbers from an early age 1 2 3 4 5 6 7 etc. We also learnt another sequence i.e. The English alphabet A B C D E F G etc.

Let's take advantage of this fact. Use the English alphabet to give a structured order to our sequence of events.

For this system we are going to create images to represent each of the first ten letters of the alphabet - A B C D E F G H I J. The human mind likes dealing with things in categories. If you were to think about the word FOOD your mind would very easily be able to think of whole variety of meats, vegetables, fruits etc.

Food makes an excellent mnemonic aid. Each food certainly has its own taste and many of them vary in colour, shape, texture and smell. So let's use food to help us visualise a group of things listed in alphabetical order. Please familiarise yourself with this list as it will play an important part in the greater scheme of things later on in the book, as well as in learning the digit sequence above:

Apricot - We could use apple but "apples" is already on another list. Someone once comically described apricots as being apples wearing suede jackets.

Banana

Carrot

Dates

Eggs

Fish

Grapes

Horseradish

Ice Cream

Jelly

Let's begin our story:

A TRAIN (142) crashed into a giant APRICOT. The impact of hitting the apricot's stone in the centre caused the train to derail and lose its load of BANANAS and MILK (357), which formed a huge white lake. Thousands of bananas could be clearly seen floating in the milk.

A CHIMPANZEE (63920) chewing a CARROT swam across and stuck a sticky brown DATE on to a pair of STAMPS (61396), which were stuck to an EGG, which hatched a SNAKE (627), which crept towards the smell of FISH frying in the FOREST (8461).

Bunches of black and green GRAPES continuously rained down from the trees but were crushed by a TANK (127) that was driven by a CLOWN (752) who was blinded by a dollop of HORSERADISH, whilst playing a TRUMPET (14391), which was covered with a scoop of ICE CREAM, that was melting over a brightly burning FLAME (853), that flickered on top of a wobbly JELLY.

In this instance the food mnemonics are not particularly important. However, they do help us gauge how far into the story we have got. If you can see an egg as you recall the story you know you have passed the halfway mark. For the next part of the story you simply look for a food beginning with the letter F. You could probably link the sequences together without using the alphabetic system but it is worth making the extra effort.

This is a deliberately tough exercise. Go through the story a couple of times and see if you can recall all 37 digits in sequence. Once you have completed this exercise you can afford to congratulate yourself.

Chapter 3

The 3rd exercise at the end of the last chapter was a deliberately tough challenge. But I'm hoping to be able to prove now how powerful your retention of memory is. Just think for a moment what you have achieved by doing the last exercise. You have memorised and recalled a sequence of 37 digits. To do this you have learnt a new system by creating 10 images (food in alphabetical order) as well as deciphering a whole host of crazy images. This was completely separate from the list of 19 items that you have learnt thus far. Yet if you were to pick any 3 of those pieces of paper numbered 1 to 19, I would not be surprised if you could recall the corresponding item to any of those numbers almost instantly, despite having completed a difficult exercise, which took some considerable time.

Let's now continue with the original list of 99 items. We have already covered items 1 to 19, so let's cover items 20 to 29. You have probably gathered that all the mnemonic words for this section will start with the letter N (well almost).

The number 20 is translated into the letters N and Z. The mnemonic word can be NOSE (again, we are concerned only with the phonetic sound as opposed to the correct spelling -

nose is pronounced as NOZE). Noses make good mnemonic aids. For some unknown reason they have comical overtones and this quirky fact can work to our advantage at some future point. We can easily imagine a nose being elongated like Pinocchio or something dribbling from the nostrils.

Let's say the 20th item on our list is the girl's name Rebecca. We shall deal with memorising names and faces in greater detail in later chapters. But in this example we are just going to learn that the 20th item on our list is the girl's name Rebecca.

There are a couple of ways of doing this. We can simply picture a girl that we already know and imagine her nose being 10 metres long. This is using existing information and exaggeration.

To add a touch humour we could make the elongated nose tie into a knot. We have a built-in mental faculty for dealing with spatial awareness and this includes shapes and patterns. If you give some of the features in your mnemonic images a few twists and turns, such as knots, then your mind will pay more attention.

However, what if Rebecca was a name that we had never heard of before? Then we have to try to visualise something that sounds very similar. Let's assume that we know that Rebecca is a girl's name. So imagine a girl with an absurdly long nose. This informs us that we are concerned with item 20. Now we are going to make that nose interact with something that sounds similar to Rebecca. Businesses spend millions on advertising their products to make them stick in our minds. Let's take advantage of their multi-million investments for free…

Reebok is a trade name with which most of us are familiar for making sports and casual wear such as trainers (soft shoes).

Fortunately, we live in the Internet age and we can easily find a whole host of images to give us ideas and inspiration for our requirements. If you are not familiar with the name Reebok simply visit a search engine and type in the words 'Reebok logo'. Company logos are another excellent mnemonic aid. Logos are deliberately designed to stick in our minds and we can easily make good use of them for the purpose of memory.

Reebok has the same first three syllables as Rebecca. Picture your imaginary girl with a smelly running shoe hanging on the end of her absurdly long nose. Imagine that her nose is so long that her arms can't reach the end of it, yet she is repulsed by the stench of the smelly footwear. See her vigorously trying to shake it off. Picture the Reebok logo on the shoe to remind you why the shoe is there.

Number 21 is translated to the letters N and T. A good mnemonic word to use is NET. In this instance picture a child's fishing or butterfly net. You may have a recollection of playing with one of these as a child. Things from our childhood have been established in our minds the longest. The longer that something has been established in our minds the better it is for attaching new information. That's why things in numbered sequence and alphabetical order are useful for the purpose of memory. We learnt counting and the alphabet in our infancy. These skills have seemingly been with us all our lives.

So let's say that the 21st item on the list is a brick. Imagine catching a brick as it flies through the air or scooping one out a pond with your child's NET. In this instance, I would choose a butterfly NET as opposed to the fishing NET. This is because a fishing NET may require us to include a scene of water, which may distract from the essential information we are trying to remember. Although I positively encourage you to create elaborate images, it is important to ensure that every feature in your image has a reason and purpose.

Feel the weight and strain this puts on the flimsy stick. Wherever possible use more than one of your imaginary senses. Although usually just visualisation is enough, using other senses will make a much stronger mnemonic image.

Think about the texture of the brick. Think about how its rough and abrasive surface could cut and break through the material of your NET. Raise your mind's curiosity of whether the brick will break all the way through the NET or just get tangled up in it.

We are fortunate enough to live in the age of film and television. There are things we see on TV frequently that our great ancestors would probably never have dreamt of. Filming techniques like zooming in and out, slow motion and changing viewing angles are common experiences for us. The amazing thing is that we can perform these techniques in our imaginations.

Take the picture of our NET and brick. Imagine looking at it from a distance of several miles and zoom in so closely you can see the tiny strands that make up the material of the NET and see the tiny grains of sand that make up the brick.

Repeat this viewing exercise from the sides, back and front, and from the top and then from the bottom. When you look at the image from the bottom, picture the brick hitting the NET and its weight pushing the NET dangerously close to your face.

Although it has taken some time to explain the techniques of zooming, slow motion and changing perspectives, performing them need take only a split second. These are techniques that are worth practising on every mnemonic image you create.

Number 22 is translated to the letters N and N. You have probably guessed by now that we can use the word NUN to make our mnemonic image. Let's say the 22nd item on our list is earrings. Simply picture a nun wearing a giant pair of earrings.

I was once giving my memory lecture and asked the students to imagine a nun wearing a giant pair of earrings. One of the students suddenly exclaimed, 'Nuns are not allowed to wear jewellery as they take a Vow of Poverty!'

I replied, 'That is a very good reason for imagining a nun wearing earrings.' If you are aware of the fact that nuns do not wear jewellery and suddenly one day you saw a nun walking along wearing a giant pair of earrings you would take a good look and probably comment on it at a later date. It would stick in your mind.

The human mind takes notice when someone or something breaks rules. In our imagination we can break any rules we like, so long as it helps us achieve our goal of remembering information. Of course, like in an earlier example, human noses cannot be physically tied into a knot but in the domain of imagination anything is possible.

Number 23 is translated into the letters N and M. The mnemonic image that uses the letters N and M is GNOME. Of course, the letter G is silent and has no significance to the information we need to recall. This is the exception that I alluded to at the beginning of the chapter.

Let's say that the 23rd item on our list is the name Robert. Again we need to find an image of something that sounds like Robert.

The word 'rabbit' has the same syllables as Robert (R - B - T). So let's use rabbit as our image to represent the name Robert. In this instance we could picture a rabbit nibbling the GNOME. It is easy for us to picture a garden scene with a GNOME and a rabbit as these two features are commonplace in such a setting.

There is another image we could create by using blending. We have established that we use rabbit because it has the same syllables as Robert, so let's use a characteristic of a rabbit and transfer it to the image of our GNOME. We have known from our childhood days that rabbits have long ears. Let's give the GNOME in our image long rabbit's ears. Blending and compounding our images gives us a tighter target to focus on. By imaging a GNOME with long rabbit's ears we do not need to see a garden setting to recall the essential information

The number 24 is translated in to the letters N and R. The mnemonic image for this example may not immediately spring to mind. However, with a little imagination we can always find something that suits our purpose.

In this instance we are going to picture an image of the Roman emperor NERO. You may recall the myth that NERO was the emperor who continued playing the violin whilst Rome burned. So that we do not get confused with any other Roman emperor, picture our Roman emperor NERO playing a violin.

Let's say that the 24th item on our list is sugar. Picture NERO playing the violin whilst Rome burns and imagine the bow of the violin puncturing a bag of sugar. Imagine the sugar trickling into the fire and fuelling the flames.

Here we can spot an opportunity to make an association to reinforce our memory. Let's make an association between a violin and sugar. The association we are looking for is sweet music. Furthermore, we could picture the bow as being similar to a cane. Now we can make a play on words - sugar cane.

Exercise 4

It is always worthwhile to scan over our mnemonic images to see if we can find any opportunity to make such associations. I found one whilst reflecting over the 9th group of numbers in the earlier mnemonic story (sequence of 37 numbers). Without physically reading the story again see if you can come up with the same connecting word. I will give you the answer at the end of this chapter but accept this fun challenge and try to spot it yourself.

The number 25 is translated into the letters N and L. The mnemonic image is that of a NAIL. A NAIL makes a good mnemonic aid as we can hang something from it or violently penetrate an article or object with it. We are now going to memorise a sentence, as opposed to just one single item. The 25th item on our list is the sentence: *King John signed the Magna Carta in 1215.*

We need to find something that we can visualise to represent the word 'king'. A crown is something that we can easily visualise as it has a very distinctive shape and can also be seen as a shiny or glittery object. We now NAIL the crown to a toilet seat. We use the image of a toilet to represent the name John - John is an American slang word for toilet. To recall the word 'signed', we can imagine a road sign being placed in the toilet. To help link the images together place the stand of the sign through the crown and into the water of the toilet.

To represent the word Magna, imagine a magnet (horse shoe shaped) attached to the sign. Then imagine the magnet attracting and pulling a cart (as if it was made of metal), which represents the word Carta. See the cart mysteriously moving towards the magnet.

To recall the figure 1215 we could imagine that the cart is carrying some TINS with TAILS (12 and 15). However, a problem may arise as we might find it difficult to decipher whether the date is 1512 or 1215. There are various ways to overcome this problem. We could place the TINS on the cart and have the TAILS dangling from the back of the cart. You should look at this image as if reading it from left to right like a book. This will indicate that the first number is 12 followed by 15. There is an opportunity here to compound TIN with TAIL. Simply picture a TIN of oxtail soup. Unfortunately a problem may arise that we might not easily identify the contents of the TIN. Although it is still worth spending a few seconds to find a fitting pun to help us recall information, even if we don't use the image of the pun in our mnemonic. Puns are another powerful tool at our disposal.

However, we can look at an alternative way of making another simple and compact image. In this instance we need to use an alternative letter for the letter T to represent 1. We can use the letter D because like the letter T it has only one vertical stroke (we will look at alternative letters in a later chapter). I'm sure you can imagine having more letters at our disposal will give us more opportunity to create mnemonic words.

Using the letters D N T and L, we can create the word dental. Unfortunately dental is not something we can immediately visualise. However, I'm sure we can all identify dental floss. Usually there is always something that we can find that we can visualise that represents our mnemonic word (remember the policeman representing the word LAW in number 5).

So let's imagine that the cart is not carrying TINS of TAILS but is tied up with dental floss. However, dental floss is quite transparent and not always clearly seen. But we can imagine the dental floss having been used for cleaning someone's teeth with blood and tiny pieces of food debris dripping from the strand of dental floss (repulsion - also blood is a good mnemonic aid as we have an inherent fear of it).

So let's refocus on our image: We picture a crown NAILed to a toilet seat with a road sign passing through it. A magnet is attached to the sign, which attracts a metal cart and wrapped round the cart is a freshly used piece of dental floss.

26 is translated into the letters N and S. We make up the mnemonic word NOOSE. It is easy to imagine something hanging in a NOOSE. Let's say the 26th item on our list is a motorbike. Simply picture the NOOSE passing through the spokes of the motorbike's front wheel. See it swinging to and fro dangling from the NOOSE's rope but also hear the sound of the motorbike's engine. Whenever you have an image of an object that has a distinctive sound, use that sound in your mnemonic image.

Try not to picture anyone riding the motorbike in your image as this may distract from the fact that we are only trying to remember the word motorbike in the 26th position. A motorbike has enough movement, sound and animation for our requirements.

The number 27 is translated into the letters N and K. Probably the one short word using the letters N and K is the word NECK, however, a NECK by itself may not be easy to visualise. So let's think of something that we can associate with the word NECK. For this we can turn to the animal kingdom and think of a giraffe. Again this is probably existing information that we have known since our childhood.

Let's say the 27th item on our list is a tomato. Think about the dark and light patterns on a giraffe's NECK and picture a bright red tomato on each dark patch of the giraffe's NECK. Also think for a moment how long it would take for a giraffe to swallow a tomato. Picture the shape of a tomato rolling down the inside of the giraffe's NECK.

Probably the one short word using the letters N and K is the word NECK, however, a NECK by itself may not be easy to visualise. So let's think of something that we can associate with the word NECK. For this we can turn to the animal kingdom and think of a giraffe. Again this is probably existing information that we have known since our childhood.

Think about the dark and light patterns on a giraffe's NECK and picture a bright red tomato on each dark patch of the giraffe's NECK. Also think for a moment how long it would take for a giraffe to swallow a tomato. Picture the shape of a tomato rolling down the inside of the giraffe's NECK.

The number 28 is translated into the letters N and F. The mnemonic image using the letters N and F is KNIFE. Let's say the 28th item on our list is bagpipes. Imagine a set of bagpipes being slashed by a KNIFE. See the gash in the tartan material and also hear the sound of the bagpipes fade as the bag collapses.

I would like to point out that the mind very quickly detects bold patterns such as tartan, plaid, checks and stripes.

The number 29 translates into the letters N and P. The mnemonic image for the letters N and P is NAPPY. This is chiefly a British term for a diaper. Idiomatic phrases from other cultures and languages can be used to our advantage, as this is often existing knowledge that we may have already made a special effort to learn. I'm sure that you probably knew the word *fromage* in our earlier example was French for cheese.

Let's say the 29th item on our list is a tomato. Imagine changing a baby's NAPPY and inside you find a squashed juicy tomato with its pips mixed up with the excrement. Although this is a disgusting, ghastly image use such emotions to your advantage. Remember that repulsion is a powerful tool.

Exercise 5

Take some more pieces of paper and number each one from 20 to 29. Add to the other pieces you made in the previous exercise numbered from 1 to 19. Randomly select one of these numbers. Translate the number to its corresponding letter or letters and then recall the mnemonic image that we have created using the letter or letters. Go through the whys and wherefores of how we created that image. Repeat the exercise until you have removed each number from the bag.

Remember that the process is in three parts:

1. Translate the numbers into mnemonic letters.

2. Recall the word or image created by those letters.

3. Finally recall the item on the list that is attached to the mnemonic image.

I am now going to give you the answer for the exercise that was set earlier. Firstly, you need to locate the 9th group of numbers. You may recall that each group of numbers was attached to a food that was listed in alphabetical order. The 9th letter of the alphabet is I and therefore you need to think of a food beginning with the letter I. In this instance, the food was Ice Cream. You may recall that the ice cream was melting on a trumpet. So think about what association you can make with ice cream and trumpet. The answer is CORNET (a cornet is a similar musical instrument to a trumpet and also a cone-shaped wafer container for ice cream).

Chapter 4

It will be of no surprise that the mnemonic words from 30 to 39 could begin with the letter M. However, you are probably so familiar with the 10 mnemonic letters that we can now learn an extended alphabet to give us further options. We have already seen some alternative letters and have put them to good use (P and B, S, SH and CH, K and C).

It will not take very long to familiarise ourselves with alternative letters for all 10 digits.

Here are the alternative letters:

1. T D

2. N H

3. M W

4. R G

5. L X Y

6. S SH CH

7. K C Q

8. F TH V PH

9. P B

10. Z J G

Let's learn the whys and wherefores of each letter of the extended Mnemonic Alphabet.

1.   T D We use the letter D for the same reason we use the letter T, i.e. it has one vertical stoke.

2.   N H The letter H is used for 2 because like the letter N it has 2 vertical strokes.

3.   M W The letter W is the digit 3 because it looks like an inverted letter M. Notice that we are making use of existing knowledge. We have already established that the letter M is the digit 3, but we are now simply inverting that image of a letter M to give us an alternative.

4.   R G We have already learnt that the digit 4 is expressed with the letter R because it is the fourth letter of the word DOOR and we use the image of DOOR because it rhymes with four.

In this instance if we are going to use the letter G. We need to find a reason to use this letter. To remember that the letter G is going to represent the digit 4 think of G-force. G-force is a phenomenon that you probably have already heard of. So again we are using existing information. The word 'force' sounds like the plural of four (fours).

However, the letter G has two sounds. For example, the letter G is pronounced differently for goat than it is for giraffe. Let's use the sound of G as in goat for number 4 (to help, mind you, goat has only four letters). We will make use of the other sounding G as in giraffe for another digit which will be explained a little later.

5.   L X Y We have already established why we use the letter L for the digit 5 (LAW). We can use the letter X to represent the digit 5 because X has a similar pattern to that which represents number 5 on dice and dominos.

We can also use the letter Y to represent the digit 5. However, we are going to have to stretch our imaginations to find a reason to use this letter. To remember why we use Y to represent the digit 5 think of the TV series *Hawaii Five-0*. In this instance the emphasis is on the Y sound of Hawaii (Hah-Y-ee) This probably seems very tenuous, but it will suffice for our purpose. Frequently these idiomatic reasons stick out like a sore thumb. The fact that they are so prominent is to our advantage.

However, the Y sound that we are looking for to represent the number 5 is the sound that is used in yacht and yoghurt.

6.   S SH CH We have already explained and used these letters in previous examples. We can also use a soft sounding C that sounds like the letter S (cigar).

7.   K C Again we have covered these two letters in earlier examples. (COW/KOW).

8.   F TH PH V We simply use these letters because they all have a similar sound to the letter F.

9.   P B We have already learnt (PEA/BEE).

Sensational Memory

0.   Z J G We have already established that the digit 0 is represented by the letter Z for zero but we can use the letter J to represent the digit 0 because J is the tenth letter in the alphabet.

We can also make use of the sound of the letter G as in giraffe. This is because the letter G in this instance sounds similar to the sound of the letter J.

We will make use of these alternative mnemonic letters in due course.

The number 30 is translated into the letters M and Z. Here we can create a mnemonic image using the letters M and Z to make the mnemonic word MAZE. For the 30th item on the list we are going to have another challenge of memorising another long sentence which is: *Stephenson's Rocket won the Rainhill Trials on 6th October 1829.*

Firstly we picture a MAZE with possibly its high hedges (Hampton Court, England has a famous MAZE and you can easily find photographs of it on the Internet to help you with your visualisation, if necessary). We now need to picture somebody called Stephen with the sun shining in his eyes (see him squinting) - it is important to make the image of Stephen and the sun interact in some way. You may not know someone called Stephen personally but there are several famous people who share that name, Stephen Spielberg, Stephen Hawking, etc. So now we have an image for Stephenson.

Imagine a rocket (see the rocket with a large number 1 written on its side - this is to represent the word won) flying towards the sun, but up into the rainy hills (see dark clouds and rain falling on the hills). To find something to represent the word trials see a sheep dog rounding up sheep (sheepdog trials).

Now we need to add images to represent the date 6th October 1829. Let's deal with 6th October first. We already have a mnemonic image for 6, which is SHOE. Now we need to find something that we can visualise that sounds like October. In this instance we can picture an octopus crawling over the rainy hills wearing large SHOES.

To remember the year 1829 we picture one end of a strand of TOFFEE coming from the SHOES, and the other end of the TOFFEE being stuck to a NAPPY.

Number 31 is translated into the letters M and T. We simply place a vowel between the two mnemonic letters to create an image of a MAT. In this instance try to picture a brown foot MAT with spiky bristles. These types of mat have a certain feel to them that has probably been familiar to us for a very long time.

Let's say the 31st item on our list is a pair of spectacles. Imagine the spectacles slightly buried in the thickness of the MAT. Furthermore, see some of those sharp bristles penetrating the glass in the frames of the spectacles.

Try to become emotionally involved with your mnemonic images. Imagine how you would feel if you had misplaced your spectacles (imagine you were dependent on your spectacles to read). Then imagine how you would you feel if you suddenly found your spectacles on a MAT and the spiky bristles had damaged your spectacles in this peculiar manner.

The number 32 is translated into the letters M and N. Here we can make a simple 3-letter mnemonic word, that being MAN. However, as people are frequently featured in our mnemonic images we need to think of a specific type of MAN to represent the number 32.

Sensational Memory

To get an established iconic image of a MAN, think of a cave MAN. This will have connotations of early MAN as opposed to just any anonymous MAN.

We can easily imagine a cave MAN wearing a loincloth and carrying a club. And we can easily picture the club interacting with an object or article that we are trying to remember.

Let's say that the 32nd item on our list is a wine bottle. Imagine our cave MAN smashing the wine bottle with his club.

You may notice that the word wine has the mnemonic letters W and N which can also represent the number 32. I have deliberately chosen a wine bottle in this example to help you establish that W can also represent the number 3.

The number 33 is translated into the letters M and M. Here we can create the mnemonic word MUMMY. Not to be confused with MOTHER but using an image of an Egyptian MUMMY. To help you reaffirm that the alternative representative letter of 3 is W, picture the MUMMY pushing a moWer (lawnmower).

The Number 34 is translated into the letters M and R. Here we can make up the mnemonic word MARROW to represent the number 34. However, you will notice that the last letter of the word MARROW is W. But in this instance we ignore the W, as it is not a prominent sounding W as in wigwam or window etc.

Let's say the 34th item on our list is a sword. Simply imagine a MARROW with its green and yellow stripes being stabbed or penetrated by a sword. Or we could see the MARROW being sliced into several pieces by a sword.

The Number 35 is translated into the letters M and L. We can create the mnemonic word MILL to represent the number 35.

- 39 -

Chris Hare

In this example we can picture a large windMILL. We can simply choose to ignore the letters w i n d and focus on the word MILL.

Let's say the 35th item on our list is a bicycle. Imagine a bicycle attached to one of the sails of the MILL (windMILL) and watch it go round and round. Here we can make another tenuous connection. WindMILLS are found in Holland were there are many bicycles.

The number 36 is translated into the letters M and S. Here we can think of a MOUSE as our mnemonic image. A MOUSE makes a good mnemonic aid as it has an iconic shape, we can easily imagine it scurrying about or gnawing and chewing something.

Let's imagine that the 36th item on our list is a piano. Simply picture a MOUSE scurrying up and down the black and white keys. To reinforce our mnemonic, hear those keys making the sound of the song *Three Blind Mice*.

Let's take a moment to think about combining and blending. If we had to memorise the number 3 6 3 1, we could simply think of a MOUSE MAT. The advantage here is that we use only one image of a MOUSE MAT as opposed to two images of a MOUSE interacting with a MAT. Ideally we need to create mnemonic images that give us the required information as quickly, clearly and as concisely as possible.

The number 37 is translated into the letters M and K. In this instance we can think of a MIKE (microphone).

Let's say the 37th item on our list is a seagull. Picture a seagull perched on a MIKE in its stand, but also hear the cry of the gull being amplified by the MIKE.

In this instance the number 38 is translated into the letters M and TH to create the mnemonic image MOTH. A MOTH is a good mnemonic aid as we can easily see it fluttering about.

Let's imagine the 38th item on our list is a blanket. In this instance try to picture a blanket that is familiar to you. A blanket with a pattern that you loosely recognise from a previous occasion. Imagine this blanket being shaken with several brightly coloured MOTHs fluttering around it.

Try not to see a person shaking the blanket, just see the act of the blanket being shaken. This is so that an unnecessary feature does not distract us in our mnemonic image.

The number 39 is translated into the letters M and P. We can create the mnemonic image of a MOP to represent the number 39.

Let's say the 39th item on our list is a cardboard box. Imagine a dripping wet MOP puncturing a cardboard box. Picture the cardboard box with a wet soggy stain where the MOP penetrates the cardboard.

Remember it is important, wherever possible, to make the information that you are trying to remember interact with your mnemonic peg.

It is worthwhile trying to find properties of things that you are trying to remember. As in the above example we can easily imagine a MOP being dripping wet, a cardboard box being punctured and the cardboard appearing soggy as a result of the contact with a wet mop.

Exercise 6

Take some more pieces of paper and number each one from 30 to 39. Add to the other pieces you made in the previous exercise numbered from 1 to 29 Randomly select one of these numbers. Translate the number to its corresponding letter or letters and then recall the mnemonic image that we have created using the letter or letters. Go through the whys and wherefores of how we created that image. Repeat the exercise until you have removed each number from the bag.

Remember that the process is in three parts:

1. Translate the numbers into mnemonic letters.

2. Recall the word or image created by those letters.

3. Finally recall the item on the list that is attached to the mnemonic image.

However, by now you should be working through the process very quickly and the items on the list will come to mind virtually simultaneously.

Exercise 7

To close this chapter I am going to leave you with a little brainteaser. Create a mnemonic image of just two words for this series of numbers: 771506. I will give you a clue by saying that the two words do have a connection. Also I have used one of our newly learned alternative Mnemonic Alphabet letters.

You may, of course, be able to create several suitable mnemonic images but just for fun see if you can pick up on the same image that I created. I will give you the answer later in the next chapter.

Chapter 5

The mnemonic images that we are going to create for the numbers 40 to 49 could all begin with the letter R. However, we will make some use of the alternative mnemonic letter G (as in goat) to represent the digit 4.

The number 40 is translated into the letters R and Z. Here we can create a mnemonic image of a ROSE (in this instance the letter S has a phonetic Z sound).

Let's look at a few alternative mnemonic images we could possibly use to represent the number 40.

We could use the letters G and G, using their two separate phonetic sounds. For example we could create a mnemonic image of a GOUGE (type of chisel). Again I would like to mention making use of Internet search engines to get defined images. Simply by taking such action in itself will help you remember. Making an extra effort frequently pays dividends.

Another example of this is if you write something down on a piece of paper, the action of writing helps you remember even if you do not refer to the piece of paper again. It's the act of taking action that makes your memory work and function well.

We could use the letters G and Z to create the mnemonic word GAUZE. However, this may not be something that we can picture in our minds immediately unless GAUZE is something you had dealings with on an everyday basis.

We could also take the letters G and Z to create the word GAZE. Although GAZE is not a noun it is possible to find something that represents the word GAZE. In this instance, we could picture a telescope, which is something that someone would GAZE through.

Remember that when we are looking at a mnemonic image that is representational we do not translate any of the mnemonic letters that might make up that word, as in our earlier example of a policeman to represent the digit 5. We actually look at the policeman so that we come up with the word LAW that gives us the mnemonic letter L.

However, it is probably best to use the image of a ROSE to represent the digits 4 and 0. Let's look at some of the reasons why. A ROSE is something that we have had established in our minds probably since our infancy. A ROSE has colour, shape, and petals that fall (movement), thorns (violence, pain and damage) and smell. A ROSE is also probably the first word that springs to mind when trying to create a mnemonic word using the letters R and Z in this system. Provided that a newly created mnemonic image is in keeping with the usual rules, the first image is more often than not the most powerful and the best option to use.

Let's say the 40th item on our list is an armchair. We could simply just picture a ROSE on an armchair, but because we specifically want to recall that the item is an armchair as opposed to any kind of chair, we shall place a ROSE on each arm of the chair. Feel yourself sitting down on the armchair and as you rest your arms you feel the ROSE thorns sticking into you and causing pain, in your arms. At a later date when you recall the mnemonic image and feel those thorns sticking in your arms and the word arm will help bring forth the word armchair.

We can reinforce our mnemonic by using some of the alternative mnemonic words we have just created (GOUGE, GAUZE and GAZE). Instead of using two or three separate images let's create one image as a collage to reinforce what we require to remember. Imagine that our armchair has ROSEs on the arms, GOUGING into the chairs material, a GAUZE seat and imagine yourself sitting in the armchair GAZING through a telescope.

However, I hasten to add that it is best to visualise an actual object as opposed to an action. In the above example it will be better to see a GOUGE as an implement interacting with the armchair as opposed to trying to remember that the thorns are GOUGING into the armchair. This is because when you reflect on the image of the thorns in the armchair the mnemonic word GOUGE may not immediately spring to mind.

Having various images to represent the same number can be very useful. This is especially true when we are memorising a series of numbers and one particular number is repeated several times. This, coupled with using the alphabetical peg system we learnt earlier, will certainly facilitate our powers of recall.

Number 41 is translated into the letters R and T or G and T. Here we have several options to create mnemonic words: RAT, GOAT or GATE. To help you establish that these images represent number 41, compact them into one scene. Imagine a GOAT head-butting a RAT against a GATE.

Whenever possible try to give alternative reasons for using an image. For example let's take the image of a GATE. Imagine a five bar gate which has four horizontal bars and one diagonal bar. The four horizontal bars can represent the number 4 and the diagonal bar can represent the number 1 (41).

Although it is not totally necessary to make alternative images it is nevertheless a good exercise and is a good habit to cultivate. With a little practice you will soon automatically spot such opportunities.

Let's say the 41st item on the list is a television. We can simply picture a goat head-butting a television and smashing the screen. Another, perhaps more surprising, image would be to imagine watching TV and suddenly see a goat's head smash through the screen from inside the TV set.

We could also picture a RAT running across the TV screen. But since our minds are subconsciously interested in shape and form imagine the rat running around the four sides of the rectangular TV screen. Perhaps also see the rat sniffing and gnawing in each corner. When using animals in mnemonic imagery try to make use of typical behaviour patterns of the animal.

To use the image of a GATE and TV imagine the screen having lines with the pattern of a five bar gate (as described earlier). Melding two images together is a very powerful memory technique. Ironically, by not actually visualising a gate but just seeing lines in a similar pattern makes a stronger mnemonic.

Number 42 is translated into the letters R or G (4) and N or H (2). Using these letters we can create the mnemonic images of RUIN and GUN.

If you take the option of a RUIN try to have a specific RUIN in mind. Try to choose a place you are familiar with. A place that you might have visited, read about or seen in a TV documentary. When you are first trying to establish a newly created image don't forget to zoom in and out and look at your image from different angles and perspectives. Look for distinguishing characteristics and features. There may be one prominent feature that stands out clearly in your mind. The RUIN you are thinking of may have an unusual type of stonework, gateway or tower. Use this particular feature to represent the number 42 and attach an image of whatever you need to remember.

A castle sprang to mind when I first thought about a ruin. But the word castle could also represent the number 765 (K S L). So I chose a specific castle for 765 and a totally different place for a RUIN to represent 42. It is worthwhile taking a little care when creating mnemonic images so that they do not get confused with something else. Try to be as specific as possible with your mnemonic images and clearly understand what they represent and why.

If you take the option of a GUN, try to think of a handgun like a Winchester Revolver. This is a classic cowboy GUN and its revolving chamber could prove useful as we can easily imagine it spinning round. Remember movement is a powerful tool in mnemonics.

We could also imagine a rifle. However, the mnemonic letters in rifle could be used to represent the number 485.

Let's say the 42nd item on our list is a filing cabinet. Simply imagine a brand new shiny filing cabinet in the middle of the grounds of a RUIN. Remember we have a process for finding the images that represent numbers. However, we may need to do something to recollect what is attached to the mnemonic image. Usually a visual image is sufficient. But movement and sound will help us to reinforce the mnemonic.

In this instance, we can imagine seeing and hearing the drawers of the filing cabinet slamming open and shut.

If we take the option of using a GUN we can imagine the drawers opening and closing rapidly. But every time we see the drawers open we see a GUN from inside the drawers and firing a loud shot.

Notice how I described the drawers opening and closing rapidly. Here we can make an association of thinking of the words "rapid fire". Although it may take a little time to read and understand such extra associations, with practice you will soon spot them naturally with ease.

Number 43 is translated into the letters R and M and G and W. Probably the best mnemonic word to create is RAM. Animals and mechanical objects with moving parts are usually the best mnemonic images to use.

We could also create the mnemonic word GUM. Here we can picture chewing GUM. However, we need to establish in our minds that we are only concerned with the letters G and M to represent the number 43. In this instance we need to ignore the adjective word "chewing" and just focus on the sound of the word GUM.

Let's say the 43rd item on our list is a fence. We can simply imagine a RAM ramming into a fence and causing damage. Because a RAM has very distinctive curly horns we could just picture a RAM's horn attached to a wooden fence. Remember that the human mind is very perceptive to specific shapes and patterns (such as stripes, curls, and geometric patterns).

We could also imagine the RAM ramming the fence with a piece of the fence stuck to one of its horns. However, also try to see a hole in the fence that is exactly the same size and shape as the piece of fence stuck to the RAM's horn, almost as if the piece of fence fitted into the fence like a jigsaw piece.

If we are going to take the GUM option, imagine someone sitting on a fence who suddenly stands up and starts walking away. Imagine that as they walk away there is a strand of GUM that is stuck to their clothes which stretches back to the fence. Picture the GUM getting longer and longer as they walk away.

We could also picture that, as the person walks away, the GUM snaps and the elasticity of the GUM springs back and causes a large splat against the fence.

The number 44 is translated into the letters R and R, G and G or any permutation of those four letters. We could create the mnemonic word RUG.

We could also use the boy's name RORY. If you are familiar with someone who has the name RORY, then that person would make a good mnemonic image for number 44.

Although names of people make useful mnemonics, I am going to suggest that you avoid using them for the time being. This is because in a later chapter we will learn a different system that uses people's names.

Let's say the 44th item on our list is a matchbox. Imagine that someone begins to shake a RUG that has a large matchbox resting on it. As the RUG is shaken you see the matches fly from the matchbox. Let's take this image a stage further and imagine that some of the matches suddenly become alight in flight and cause the RUG to catch fire. Notice that I ask you to imagine that only some of the matches are alight in flight. This is so that you can also picture some of the matches that are not alight. We can then emphasise on the matches themselves, as opposed to flames, sparks or fire. However, remember to keep an image of the matchbox in view throughout your mnemonic scene.

If you are going to use the option of using the image of someone called RORY, simply imagine RORY striking matches from a matchbox. In this instance, remember to hear the sound of a match striking against the box. See RORY continuously taking matches out of the matchbox and striking them. This is so we can give more emphasis to the word matchbox as opposed to the word matches.

The number 45 can be translated into the letters R or G (4) along with the letters L, X or Y (5). We can create the mnemonic word ROLL (as in bread ROLL)

A ROLL makes a useful mnemonic because we can imagine rolling a ROLL or placing something inside it as if to make a sandwich.

By using the letters G and L we can also use the word GLOW. In this instance we could picture a GLOWworm. Simply picture the worm glowing. Here again we are simply using something to represent the word GLOW to represent the number 45.

Let's say the 45th item on our list is a book. We can imagine ourselves taking a bite of a ROLL that has a book inside it as opposed to a usual edible filling. Here we can make another extended association by thinking of the word "digest" (digesting food and digesting a book).

If we use the option of a GLOWworm we can picture some worms that are glowing as they eat into a book. Again here we can think about another extended association by thinking of a bookworm.

The number 46 can be translated into the letters R or G (4) along with the letters S, SH or CH. (6). We can create the mnemonic image of RICE (in this instance we are using a soft C which sounds like the letter S to represent the number 6).

By using the mnemonic letter G and S, we can create a mnemonic image of a GOOSE.

Let's say the 46th item on our list is a cigarette. Picture somebody throwing rice at someone smoking a cigarette. Imagine that the person is throwing the rice because they don't like the smell of tobacco. It is a good idea to give reason and purpose to your imagery even though your image might be quite bizarre.

If we take the option of using the mnemonic image of a GOOSE, simply picture a GOOSE smoking a cigarette. We could take this another step further. One of the features of geese is that they have long necks. Imagine that our GOOSE has got a cigarette in place of a neck. This is a similar technique to that which we used for item number 15 on our list.

The number 47 translates into the letters R or G (4) and K, C or Q (7). Using the mnemonic letters R and K we can form the mnemonic image of a RAKE (garden rake).

Admittedly it is quite difficult to think of a mnemonic word using the other alternative mnemonic letters. However, not to be defeated, I came up with an image of Saddam Hussein the notorious IRAQI leader.

Let's say the 47th item on our list is a pair of curtains. We can easily imagine a pair of stage curtains at a theatre and a RAKE poking through the gap in the centre. We can also make another association as the word RAKE is used to describe a slope on a stage.

If we take the IRAQI option you can imagine Saddam Hussein repeatedly opening and closing a pair of curtains.

The number 48 is translated into the letters R or G (4) and F, V, or TH (8). Using the letters R and F we can make the mnemonic image of a ROOF. In this instance picture a ROOF with a chimney. This is so that we can place an item against the chimney or have something coming out of the chimney. Chimneys can easily be associated with rooftops.

Using the letters G and F we can create a mnemonic image of GOOFY (famous Disney cartoon character).

Let say that the 48th item on our list is a teddy bear. Imagine a teddy bear has climbed onto a ROOF and is pulling down the chimney brick by brick.

Sensational Memory

Taking the option of using GOOFY simply imagine GOOFY dancing on a ROOF with a teddy bear in his goofy teeth.

The number 49 translates into the letters R or G (4) and P and B (9). Using the letters R and P we can create the mnemonic image of a ROPE.

We can make an alternative image using the letters R and B to create the mnemonic image of a ROBE.

Let's say the 49th item on our list is a handbag. Imagine the handbag has a broken strap that has been replaced by a ROPE.

If we take the option of using the mnemonic image of a ROBE simply picture someone wearing a ROBE swinging a handbag.

I am now going to give you the answer to Exercise 7. The mnemonic image I created to remember the numbers 771506 was the two words COCKTAIL JUICE.

Exercise 8

Take some more pieces of paper and number each one from 40 to 49. Add to the other pieces you made in the previous exercise numbered from 1 to 39. Randomly select one of these numbers. Translate the number to its corresponding letter or letters and then recall the mnemonic image that we have created using the letter or letters. Go through the whys and wherefores of how we created that image. Repeat the exercise until you have removed each number from the bag.

Exercise 9

Create mnemonic images using one or more of the alternative mnemonic letters for numbers 1 to 39. I will give you my alternative images later in the next chapter. However, your list of mnemonic images need not match my list.

The mnemonic image that I came up with for 771506 in Exercise 7 was COCKTAIL JUICE. Do not worry if you did not come up with these two words it is just a fun exercise. It is more important that you create a mnemonic image that works for you. However, you may have noticed that some mnemonic words hold more information than others. As in the cocktail juice example the word cocktail contains the digits 7715 and the word juice the digits 06.

Chapter 6

In this chapter, I shall give only one example mnemonic word for each number from 50 to 59. However, there will be an exercise at the end of the chapter asking you to create alternative images using the other letters.

Number 50 is translated into the mnemonic letters L X Y (5) and Z J G (0). Using the mnemonic letters L and G we can create the mnemonic image of a LODGE (we can afford to ignore the letter D as it is virtually silent).

Let's say the 50th item on the list is a wallet. Simply imagine a wallet outside a LODGE. We can reinforce the mnemonic by substituting the door of the lodge with a giant sized wallet. Picture the door of the lodge as a huge wallet that opens and closes automatically. Picture the contents of the wallet (cash, credit cards etc.) but keep in view the lodge in the background.

Number 51 is translated into the mnemonic letters L X Y (5) and T or D (1). Using the mnemonic letters Y and T we can create the mnemonic image of a YACHT.

Let's say the 51st item on the list is a washing machine. Picture a YACHT sailing over breaking waves with a washing machine on top of the yacht's triangular sails. Imagine the washing machine busily vibrating as its moving parts spin round. Picture soapsuds pouring from the machine and slithering down the yacht's sails.

Number 52 is translated into the mnemonic letters L X Y (5) and N or H (2). Using the mnemonic letters L and N we can create the mnemonic image LION.

Let's say the 52nd item on the list is a newspaper. Simply imagine a LION mauling a newspaper. Hear the lion roar and hear the paper being torn into shreds

Number 53 is translated into the mnemonic letters L X Y (5) and M or W (3). Using the letters L and M we can create the mnemonic image of a LAMB.

Let's say the 53rd item on the list is a stilt walker. In this instance, we can look at the characteristics of the thing we are trying to remember (stilt walker) and the mnemonic image that represents 53 (LAMB). The stilt walker is very tall and a frisky lamb likes to jump. Imagine the lamb jumping so high that it knocks the stilt walker's hat off.

It is worthwhile spending a few seconds to see if you can find some correlation between the properties and characteristics of the images you are trying to link together. Look for correlations in movement, colour, size and shape.

Number 54 is translated into the mnemonic letters L X Y (5) and R or G (4). Using the letters L and G we can create a mnemonic image of a LOG.

Let's say the 54th item on the list is a bed sheet. Simply imagine a log rolling along the four sides of a rectangular bed sheet. Remember, the human mind instinctively likes to deal with shape and form. Logs are usually sawn pieces of wood so imagine a trail of sawdust in the trail of the log's path.

Try to picture a bed sheet that you are familiar with. You might own a bed sheet with a distinctive pattern. Remember to zoom in and use slow motion in your images. See those tiny specks of sawdust flying from the log and landing on the bed sheet.

Zooming in and using slow motion is useful if you are experiencing a problem in grasping a memorable image.

Number 55 is translated into the mnemonic letters L X or Y. By repeating the L we can create a mnemonic image of a LILO (an inflatable rubber or plastic type of mattress). A lilo makes a good mnemonic because it can float on water and it can also be punctured.

Let's say the 55th item on the list is a hacksaw. Imagine someone floating on a lilo in a swimming pool. Picture sawing into the lilo causing it to burst and sink in the water. Make sure you picture the shiny metal of the saw and see the sharp teeth cutting into the lilo's fabric. See bubbles in the water where the air is leaking from the lilo.

Number 56 is translated into the mnemonic letters L X Y (5) and S SH or CH (6). Using the letters L and SH we can create a mnemonic image of a LEASH.

Let's say the 56th item on the list is a basket. Imagine a basket attached to a leash. However, since a leash is an implement for keeping a dog under control, stretch your imagination by making the basket behave like a ferocious dog. See the basket pulling on the leash and jumping up and down, and hear it snarl like an angry dog.

Number 57 is translated into the mnemonic letters L X Y (5) and K or C (6). Using the letters L and K we can create a mnemonic image of a LAKE.

Let's say the 57th item on the list is an igloo. Imagine an igloo floating but melting in the warm waters of a lake. Whenever you create a bizarre image (let's be frank, an igloo is hardly likely to be seen floating on a lake) make your images interact with each other. Ask yourself, 'What would happen if...'

Number 58 is translated into the mnemonic letters L X Y (5) and F TH PH V (8). Using the letters L and F we can create a mnemonic image of a LEAF.

Let's say the 58th item on the list is a rollercoaster. Imagine the passengers on the rollercoaster travelling through a shower of leaves. See the passengers trying to wave the leaves from in front of their faces as they scream. Sometimes rollercoasters are called "white knuckle rides". See leaves settling on the white knuckles of the passengers.

Number 59 is translated into the mnemonic letters L X Y (5) and P B (9). Using the letters L and B we can create the mnemonic image of a LAB (laboratory). Informal abbreviations grant us a licence of which we make good use.

Let's say the 59th item on our list is a tractor. Picture a scientific lab with an assortment of test tubes containing various chemical liquids. Then suddenly imagine that a tractor smashes into the test tubes and the chemical liquids splash on to the tractor and have a corrosive effect on the body of the tractor.

I am now going to give you a list of the alternative mnemonic letters for numbers 1 to 39 (Exercise 9). The mnemonic images may differ from your own but this will not matter so long as your images work for the purpose of recalling information:

1. D Doe (a deer, a female deer)

2. H Hoe (garden tool)

3. W Weigh (kitchen scales - representative image)

4. G Guy (Guy Fawkes or think of someone called Guy)

5. X Axe

6. S Sow (a pig, a female pig)

7. K Key

8. V View (think of a favourite view that you have already established in your memory)

9. B Bee (as already discussed)

10. TJ Taj Mahal

11. TD Toad

12. DN Dune

13. DM Dummy

14. DG Dog

15. DL Doll

16. D SH Dish
17. DK Duck
18. DV Dove
19. TB Tub
20. HG Hedge
21. HT Hut
22. HN Hen
23. HM Ham
24. HG Hog
25. HL Hail
26. H S Hose
27. HK Hook
28. HV Hive
29. HP Hippy
30. MG Mage (archaic word for magician)
31. MD Mud
32. WN Wine
33. WM Worm (ignoring the letter R as it is not rolling)
34. MG Mug

35. WL Willow

36. M CH Match

37. WK Wok

38. WF Wife (picture a bride)

39. WB Web (spider's web)

Exercise 10

Take some more pieces of paper and number each one from 50 to 59. Add to the other pieces you made in the previous exercise numbered from 1 to 49. Randomly select one of these numbers. Translate the number to its corresponding letter or letters and then recall the mnemonic image that we have created using the letter or letters. Go through the whys and wherefores of how we created that image. Repeat the exercise until you have removed each number from the bag.

Exercise 11

Create mnemonic images using one or more of the alternative mnemonic letters for numbers 50 to 59. I will give you my alternative images later in the next chapter. Again, your list of mnemonic images need not match my list.

Chapter 7

Number 60 is translated into the mnemonic letters S SH CH (6) and Z J G (0). Using the letters CH and using the S that has a Z sound we can create a mnemonic image of CHEESE. Edam cheese makes a good mnemonic image as it has a distinctive red peel.

Let's say the 60th item on the list is a pencil. Simply imagine a pencil being used as a cocktail stick, penetrating right through a piece of cheese.

Number 61 is translated into the mnemonic letters S SH CH (6) and T D (1). Using the letters SH and D we can create the mnemonic image of a SHED. However, make sure that the shed you have in mind looks totally different from a hut (21). Remember to try to make use of images that are already established in your mind.

Let's say the 61st item on the list is an electrical plug. Simply imagine a gigantic electrical plug plugged into the wall of a wooden shed. Imagine that the plug is almost as large as the shed's wall.

Sensational Memory

Change the perspective of your view and see the metal prongs of the plug pushing into the wood. See the plug automatically plugging and unplugging in the shed in slow motion. See a blue electrical flash between the plug and the shed.

Number 62 is translated into the mnemonic letters S SH CH (6) and N H (2). Using the letters CH and N we can make a mnemonic image of a CHAIN.

Let's say the 62nd item on the list is a coffin. Simply imagine a coffin being lowered into a grave on a chain. Or see a coffin lid being lifted off by a chain.

Number 63 is translated into the mnemonic letters S SH CH (6) and M W (3). Using the letters S and M we can create a mnemonic image of a SUMO wrestler.

Let's say the 63rd item on the list is a candle. Simply imagine a sumo wrestler holding a lighted candle. Picture the sumo puffing and blowing trying to blow the flame out.

Number 64 is translated into the mnemonic letters S SH CH (6) and R G (4). Using the letters CH and R we can create a mnemonic image of a CHAIR. Again try to picture a chair with which you are familiar. An office swivel chair would make a good mnemonic.

Let's say the 64th item on the list is a diary. Simply imagine a chair swivel round slowly and there resting at an angle of 45 degrees between the seat and the back of a chair is an open diary

When creating mnemonic images give yourself specific information (e.g. the diary is at 45 degrees or whatever position you want to put it). The fact that you made an extra effort to give detail will help your power of recall.

Number 65 is translated into the mnemonic letters S SH CH (6) and L X Y (5). Using the letters SH and L we can create a mnemonic image of a SHELL.

Let's say the 65th item on the list is a flute. Simply imagine someone playing a flute that has a shell hanging off the end of it. A flute is a wind instrument that is played at right angles. Picture the flute player looking to his right as if distracted by a shell swinging at the end of the flute. Remember that the human mind is sensitive to and conscious of direction.

Number 66 is translated into the mnemonic letters S SH CH (6) and a repetition of any of those letters to represent the second 6. Using the letters CH and repeating them we can create a mnemonic image of a CHURCH. It might be preferable to think of a church with a steeple.

Let's say the 66th item on the list is a hairbrush. Imagine a very tall giant with a huge hairbrush, brushing the spire of the church. In this instance, do not focus on the giant, as it will distract you from what you need to recall. Zoom in on the bristles of the hairbrush as it strokes the stonemasonry of the steeple. Zoom in and out a couple of times to keep the church in view.

Number 67 is translated into the mnemonic letters S SH CH (6) and K C (7). Using the letters S and K we can create the mnemonic image of a SOCK.

Let's say the 67th item on the list is a horse. Imagine a horse jumping and as it is in full flight picture four different brightly coloured socks on each of its legs. Giving a mnemonic image an order or pattern with variation (e.g. four different colours) will help us detect the information that we are looking for more quickly.

Number 68 is translated into the mnemonic letters S SH CH (6) and F V TH PH (8). Using the letters S and F we can create the mnemonic image of a SOFA.

Let's say the 68th item on the list is an envelope. Picture an open envelope with the apex of the flap stuck to the sofa. But imagine that the envelope is hinged at that point and is swinging side to side like a pendulum. Remember to zoom in and out of the entire image to keep both the sofa and envelope in view.

It is always worthwhile creating bizarre mnemonic images but remember to use logic and sense of purpose within the image itself.

Number 69 is translated into the mnemonic letters S SH CH (6) and P B (9). Using the letters S and P we can create a mnemonic image of SOUP. However, it is important to think of a liquid substance that you can easily recognise as soup. Possibly tomato soup has the most distinctive and bold colour.

Let's say the 69th item on the list is a helicopter. Imagine a helicopter crashing into a sea of tomato soup. As the helicopter submerges in the soup picture the rotors continuing to spin and cause the soup to be sprayed into the air.

Exercise 12

Take some more pieces of paper and number each one from 60 to 69. Add to the other pieces you made in the previous exercise numbered from 1 to 59. Randomly select one of these numbers. Translate the number to its corresponding letter or letters and then recall the mnemonic image that we have created using the letter or letters. Go through the whys and wherefores of how we created that image. Repeat the exercise until you have removed each number from the bag.

Exercise 13

Create mnemonic images using one or more of the alternative mnemonic letters for numbers 60 to 69. I will give you my alternative images later in the next chapter. Again, your list of mnemonic images need not match my list.

I am now going to give you a list of the alternative mnemonic letters for numbers 50 to 59 (Exercise 11). The mnemonic images may differ from your own but this will not matter so long as your images work for the purpose of recalling information:

50. YL Yule (Christmas scene)

51. LT Light

52. YH Yahoo (Here I use a representational figure of a cowboy).

53. XM Exam (recall a scene where you took an examination - maybe picture a small singular desk).

54. YR Euro (A monetary unit in Europe. In this instance the letters e and u form a phonetic Y sound to represent 5).

55. Y Y Yoyo

56. L CH Loch (Scottish lake but use a representational figure of the Loch Ness Monster, this will prevent confusion with the word lake which represents 57).

57. YK Yolk (fried egg).

58. L TH Lathe

59. XP Expo (A common abbreviation for an exposition or a public exhibition).

Chapter 8

Number 70 is translated into the mnemonic letters K C Q (7) and Z J G (0). Using the letters C and G we can create a mnemonic image of a CAGE.

Let's say the 70th item on the list is an onion. Imagine an onion squashed between the bars of a cage. Picture the bars bending to the outline of the onion.

Number 71 is translated into the mnemonic letters K C Q (7) and T D (1). Using the letters K and T we can create a mnemonic image of a KITE.

Let's say the 71st item on the list is a wristwatch. Imagine a flying kite but also picture several wristwatches evenly spaced along the string of the kite. Notice that I used the words 'evenly spaced'. Remember the human mind is sensitive to order and pattern. Zoom up and down the kite's string bringing the kite into full view.

Number 72 is translated into the mnemonic letters K C Q (7) and N H (2). Using the letters C and N we can create a mnemonic image of a CANE. Picture an old man with a cane.

Canes are easily associated with old men who use them as a walking aid. This will give us an opportunity to animate the mnemonic image.

Let's say the 72nd item on the list is a hot air balloon. Picture an old man dangling from the basket of the hot air balloon by the hooked top of his cane. Place yourself in the poor unfortunate's position for a few moments.

Number 73 is translated into the mnemonic letters K C Q (7) and M W (3). Using the letters K and W we can create a mnemonic image of a KIWI. A Kiwi is a rare native bird of New Zealand. Natives of New Zealand are nicknamed Kiwis. New Zealand has an international rugby team that play in an All Black strip. If you are familiar with this image then you could use it to represent 73. Here again I am drawing on existing knowledge and finding a representational image.

Let's say the 73rd item on the list is a giraffe. Picture an All Black rugby player grabbing a giraffe around the neck.

Number 74 is translated into the mnemonic letters K C Q (7) and R G (4). Using the letters C and R we can create a mnemonic image of a CROW (ignore the letter w as it is not a prominent sound).

Let's say the 74th item on the list is a golf ball. Simply picture a crow flying off with a white golf ball in its beak.

Number 75 is translated into the mnemonic letters K C Q (7) and L X Y (5). Using the letters C and L we can create a mnemonic image of COAL. To make the image stronger we can imagine the black coal burning and glowing red. Remember the human mind is sensitive to things that shine or glow.

Let's say the 75th item on the list is a pair of white trousers. Imagine yourself wearing a pair of white trousers and putting a burning piece of coal in your trouser pocket. See the piece of coal burning through the fabric and feel the heat on your leg.

Number 76 is translated into the mnemonic letters K C Q (7) and S SH CH (6). Using the letters C and SH we can create a mnemonic image of CASH.

Let's say the 76th item on the list is a mushroom. Simply see a mushroom growing in a pile of cash.

Number 77 is translated into the mnemonic letters K C Q (7) and repeated again to make the second 7. Using the letters C and K we can create a mnemonic image of a CAKE.

Let's say the 77th item on the list is a knitting needle. Simply picture a knitting needle penetrating a cake. Imagine yourself pushing the knitting needle through the cake several times from different angles. See some of the sponge and crumbs on the knitting needle.

Number 78 is translated into the mnemonic letters K C Q (7) and F V TH PH. Using the letters C and F we can create a mnemonic image of COFFEE. Coffee makes a good mnemonic as we can see it as dark granules or as a hot liquid.

Let's say the 78th item on the list is a bottle. Picture yourself pouring teaspoonfuls of coffee granules into a bottle. Imagine a clear bottle so you can see the coffee granules inside.

Number 79 is translated into the mnemonic letters K C Q (7) and P B (9). Using the letters C and P we can create a mnemonic image of a CAP.

Let's say the 79th item on the list is a tortoise. Simply see a tortoise crawling along with a cap on its back.

Exercise 14

Take some more pieces of paper and number each one from 70 to 79. Add to the other pieces you made in the previous exercise numbered from 1 to 69. Randomly select one of these numbers. Translate the number to its corresponding letter or letters and then recall the mnemonic image that we have created using the letter or letters. Go through the whys and wherefores of how we created that image. Repeat the exercise until you have removed each number from the bag.

Exercise 15

Create mnemonic images using one or more of the alternative mnemonic letters for numbers 70 to 79. I will give you my alternative images later in the next chapter. Again, your list of mnemonic images need not match my list.

I am now going to give you a list of the alternative mnemonic letters for numbers 60 to 69 (Exercise 13). The mnemonic images may differ from your own but this will not matter so long as your images work for the purpose of recalling information:

60. S S Sousa (Sousaphone) in this instance the second s is pronounced as a z.

61. ST Soot.

62. SN Sun

63. SH M Shammy (shammy leather)

64. SR Sari

65. SL Sleigh

66. SS Sauce (tomato ketchup)

67. CH K Chick

68 CH F Chief (Red Indian Chief)

69 SH P Ship

CHAPTER 9

Number 80 is translated into the mnemonic letters F V TH PH (8) and Z J G. Using the letters F and Z we can create a mnemonic image of a FEZ.

Let's say the 80th item on the list is a broomstick. Simply picture a FEZ nesting on top of a broomstick handle. Zoom out to make sure you can see the whole of the broomstick as well as the FEZ.

Number 81 is translated into the mnemonic letters F V TH PH (8) and T D (1). Using the letters F and T we can create a mnemonic image of a FIGHT. However, in this instance picture a boxing ring. We can easily associate a boxing ring with the word FIGHT. A boxing ring with its raised platform surrounded by ropes is a very distinctive image.

Let's say the 81st item on the list is an umbrella. Picture two boxers in the ring each holding an open umbrella with their boxing glove.

Number 82 is translated into the mnemonic letters F V TH PH (8) and N H (2). Using the letters F and N we can create a mnemonic image of a FAN. In this instance, let's imagine an electric FAN, one that changes direction whilst on a stand.

Let's say the 82nd item on the list is a goldfish. See several goldfish being tossed in the air current created by the electric FAN. Focus on that image for a few seconds and imagine the sound of the FAN and feel what it must be like for the goldfish.

Whenever you have a sense of danger in your mnemonic images it is worthwhile imagining how the victim might be feeling.

Number 83 is translated into the mnemonic letters F V TH PH (8) and M W (3). Using the letters F and M we can create a mnemonic image of FOAM.

Let's say the 83rd item on the list is a pencil sharpener. Simply picture a pencil sharpener floating on some white frothy FOAM. But also see some pencil shavings coming from the pencil sharpener that fall into the FOAM. Whenever you create a mnemonic of an object that has a specific purpose, use that purpose in your imagery.

If you were to see some pencil shavings it would not be wrong to assume a pencil sharpener may have been used. Those tiny flecks of shaving FOAM may just trigger off a successful recall.

Number 84 is translated into the mnemonic letters F V TH PH (8) and R G (4). Using the letters F and R we can create a mnemonic image of a FAIRY.

Let's say the 84th item on the list is a potato. Imagine a FAIRY standing on a potato. Picture the FAIRY walking on the potato but as she walks she causes the potato to roll under her feet. Remember to try to create action and movement whenever possible.

Number 85 is translated into the mnemonic letters F V TH PH (8) and L X Y (5). Using the letters F and X we can create a mnemonic image of a FOX.

Let's say the 85th item on the list is a tablecloth. We could simply picture a FOX with a tablecloth in its mouth. However, tablecloths do have a purpose. So let's put our tablecloth on a table and place some crockery and cutlery on the tablecloth. Now see the FOX run along and pull the tablecloth with its teeth. It's not difficult to imagine the chaos this would cause. Imagine how you would feel if you had just laid that table.

Number 86 is translated into the mnemonic letters F V TH PH (8) and S SH CH (5). Using the letters TH and CH we can create a mnemonic image of a THATCH (THATCHed cottage).

Let's say the 86th item on the list is a swimming pool. Imagine a THATCHed cottage with a swimming pool built into the roof. Focus on the contrasting colours of the blue swimming pool and the dark brown THATCH. See a few bits of THATCH floating in the pool.

Number 87 is translated into the mnemonic letters F V TH PH (8) and K C (5). Using the letters F and K we can create a mnemonic image of a FORK.

Let's say the 87th item on the list is a tyre. Imagine a FORK puncturing a tyre. To give the image a bit more action, imagine stabbing the tyre a few times with the FORK.

Number 88 is translated into the mnemonic letters F V TH PH (8) and repeated again to make the second 8. Using the letters TH and F we can create a mnemonic image of a THIEF.

However, in this instance use a classic image of a THIEF wearing a mask and carrying a bag with 'swag' written on it.

Let's say the 88th item on the list is a chocolate bar. Imagine a THIEF putting several chocolate bars into his swag bag. Picture a brand of chocolate that you are familiar with.

Number 89 is translated into the mnemonic letters F V TH PH (8) and P B (9). Using the letters F and B we can create a mnemonic image of a FOB (type of watch worn by nurses).

Let's say the 89th item on the list is a T-shirt. Imagine putting on a T-shirt (a T-shirt that you are familiar with) and as you pull it over your head you can feel a small weight on the garment. As you look down to the left breast you can see a FOB watch pinned to your T-shirt.

Exercise 16

Take some more pieces of paper and number each one from 80 to 89. Add to the other pieces you made in the previous exercise numbered from 1 to 79. Randomly select one of these numbers. Translate the number to its corresponding letter or letters and then recall the mnemonic image that we have created using the letter or letters. Go through the whys and wherefores of how we created that image. Repeat the exercise until you have removed each number from the bag.

Exercise 17

Create mnemonic images using one or more of the alternative mnemonic letters for numbers 80 to 89. I will give you my alternative images later in the next chapter. Again, your list of mnemonic images need not match my list.

I am now going to give you a list of the alternative mnemonic letters for numbers 70 to 79 (Exercise 15). The mnemonic images may differ from your own but this will not matter so long as your images work for the purpose of recalling information:

70. KG Keg (beer barrel)

71. CT CAT

72. KN Ken

73. CM Comb

74. CG Cog

75. CX Cox (rowing boat)

76. CS Case

77. C CK Cuckoo

78. CV Cave

79. CB Cob (corn on the cob or a male swan).

Chapter 10

Number 90 is translated into the mnemonic letters P B (9) and Z J G (0). Using the letters P and Z we can create a mnemonic image of a PIZZA.

Let's say the 90th item on the list is a strawberry. We could simply picture a strawberry on a PIZZA. However, we can reinforce the image by imagining a round-shaped PIZZA with a triangular slice removed from it. If we now place a strawberry in the triangular space we will reinforce our mnemonic.

This works because our mind naturally detects shapes like triangles. We are also familiar with the idea of a PIZZA with a slice having been removed. We are not so familiar with a strawberry being placed in that space. This element of surprise makes our mind pay attention.

Number 91 is translated into the mnemonic letters P B (9) and T D (1). Using the letters P and T we can create a mnemonic image of a POT. Try to think of a POT that you have in your home. Every time you see that POT just think to yourself, 91. This applies to every object that you may have used as a mnemonic image.

Whenever you see a set of numbers (e.g. a car number plate) recall the mnemonic images that represent those numbers. It will not be long before the mnemonic images come to you involuntarily.

Let's say the 91st item on the list is a tennis racquet. Usually a tennis racquet is larger than what we might perceive as a POT. We could exaggerate the size of our POT so that it can accommodate a tennis racquet. However, we would get a better mnemonic image if we see our POT being hit by the tennis racquet. In this instance we are using movement and action.

We could also imagine our POT shattering as it hits the ground. Whenever we witness damage, we instinctively look for its cause. In this case we would recall the POT being struck by a tennis racquet.

The number 92 is translated into the mnemonic letters P B (9) and N H (2). Using the letters P and N we can create the mnemonic image of a PONY. We could create a mnemonic image of a PEN, but it is better to think of something that can be animated. A PONY is more versatile and will give us several options.

Let's say the 92nd item on our list is a kettle. Simply imagine a PONY carrying a steaming kettle by the handle in its teeth. Zoom in and out a few times to view the entire scene and details.

The number 93 is translated into the mnemonic letters P B (9) and M W (3). Using the letters B and M we can create a mnemonic image of a BOMB. In this instance we can picture a cartoon type BOMB (i.e. a cannon ball shape BOMB with a fizzing, burning fuse). Otherwise, unless you have some sort of military experience, you may not be au fait with an actual BOMB.

Let's say the 93rd item on our list is toothpaste. Imagine that you are squirting toothpaste around the circumference of your imaginary BOMB. As you imagine yourself doing this get a sense of how potentially dangerous this bizarre act would be. Again, use a tube of toothpaste that you are familiar with and see the trade name and colourings on the tube. Ideally, striped toothpaste would make an even more powerful mnemonic image. Remember that the human mind quickly detects patterns such as stripes.

The number 94 is translated into the mnemonic letters P B (9) and R G (4). Using the letters B and G we can create the mnemonic image of a BAG. In this instance picture a paper BAG because a paper BAG will rip or tear if an object is sharp or heavy.

Let's say the 94th item on our list is a paintbrush. Imagine a wet, dripping paintbrush being placed into a paper BAG. However, try to see the paint being absorbed by the BAG or even see blobs of paint seeping through the BAG and dropping onto the floor.

It is worthwhile becoming emotionally involved with your mnemonic images. For example, if you were concerned about paint dripping from a brush and you were to place it in a paper BAG but the paint still caused a mess, this would instinctively evoke a sensation of concern.

The number 95 is translated into the mnemonic letters P B (9) and L X Y (5). Using the letters B and X we can create a mnemonic image of a BOX. For similar reasons for using a paper bag, think of a cardboard BOX.

Let's say the 95th item on our list is shampoo. Simply imagine pouring from a bottle of shampoo onto the surface of a cardboard BOX. Then imagine yourself creating a lather with the shampoo as if you were massaging your scalp with your fingers. However, keep the shampoo and the cardboard BOX in view throughout the scene.

The number 96 is translated into the mnemonic letters P B (9) and S SH and CH (6). Using the letters B and S we can create the mnemonic image of a BUS. You may think of the famous London red double-decker BUSes, which will make an ideal mnemonic.

Let's say the 96th item on the list is a cardigan. Imagine a huge cardigan wrapped around a BUS. However, imagine the cardigan being tight-fitting and putting a huge strain on the buttons. Picture some of the buttons breaking free from the cardigan.

The number 97 is translated into the mnemonic letters P B (9) and K C (7). Using the letters B and K we can create the mnemonic image of a BOOK. Again, try to have a specific book that you are familiar with in mind.

Let's say the 97th item on the list is a roll of toilet paper. Simply imagine a toilet roll squashed between the pages of a BOOK. If the object you are trying to remember is malleable try to make use of this property whenever possible.

The number 98 is translated into mnemonic letters P B (9) and F V TH PH (8). Using the letters B and TH we can create the mnemonic image of a BATH.

Let's say the 98th item on our list is a cushion. Simply imagine yourself sat in the BATH with a cushion. Picture yourself picking up the cushion and squeezing out the soapy liquid that it has absorbed.

The number 99 is translated into the mnemonic letters P B (9) and repeated again to represent the second 9. Using the letters P and P we can create a mnemonic image of a PIPE (smoking).

Let's say the 99th item on the list is an ironing board. Simply imagine someone tapping a smouldering PIPE onto an ironing board. Picture some of the PIPE's contents spilling onto the ironing board and burning its surface.

Exercise 18

Take some more pieces of paper and number each one from 90 to 99. Add to the other pieces you made in the previous exercise numbered from 1 to 89. Randomly select one of these numbers. Translate the number to its corresponding letter or letters and then recall the mnemonic image that we have created using the letter or letters. Go through the whys and wherefores of how we created that image. Repeat the exercise until you have removed each number from the bag.

Exercise 19

Create mnemonic images using one or more of the alternative mnemonic letters for numbers 90 to 99. I will give you my alternative images later in the next chapter. Again, your list of mnemonic images need not match my list.

I am now going to give you a list of the alternative mnemonic letters for numbers 80 to 89 (Exercise 17). The mnemonic images may differ from your own but this will not matter so long as your images work for the purpose of recalling information:

80. FG Fudge

81. VD Video

82. VN Van

83. FM Fume (cloud of smoke)

84. FG Fog

85. FL File

86. FS Fuse

87. VK Vicky (girl's name)

88. F TH Feather

89. FP Fop (a man who is excessively concerned with fashion and elegance)

Chapter 11

Occasionally we may need to memorise a series of numbers beginning with the digit 0, so now let's create mnemonic images to represent 00 to 09.

Number 00 is translated into the mnemonic letters Z J G S (0) and repeated again to represent the second 0. Using the letters J and S we can create a mnemonic image of JAWS. In this instance we can think of the giant shark that featured in the popular film *JAWS*.

If you wish you can use the image for 00 to represent the number 100.

Let's make another alternative mnemonic image for 00 by using J and G and think of the mnemonic image of a JUDGE.

If you have completed all the exercises thus far you will have 200 images. Your first list can represent numbers 1 to 100 and your alternative images can represent 101 to 200.

For the sake of completion let's create mnemonic images and alternative mnemonic images from 01 to 09.

01 is translated in to the mnemonic letters Z J G S (0) and T D (1). Using the letters J and T we can create the mnemonic image of a JET. Using the letters Z and T we can create the mnemonic image of a ZIT (teenager spot/acne).

02 is translated into the mnemonic letters Z J G S (0) and N H (2). Using the letters G and N we can create the mnemonic image of GIN (bottle of). Using the letters J and N we can create the mnemonic image of a girl called JUNE.

03 is translated into the mnemonic letters Z J G S (0) and M W (3). Using the letters J and M we can create of the mnemonic image of JAM. Using the letters J and W we can think of a mnemonic image of a JEW (a Hasidic Jew). Hasidic Jews have a very distinctive traditional dress.

04 is translated into the letters Z J G S (0) and R G (4). Using the letters J and R we can create the mnemonic image of a JAR. Using the letters J and G we can create the mnemonic image of a JUG.

05 is translated into the mnemonic letters Z J G S (0) and L X Y (5). Using the letters Z and L we can create the mnemonic image of a ZULU. And using the letters G and L we can create the mnemonic image of GEL.

06 is translated into the mnemonic letters Z J G S (0) and S SH C CH (6). Using the letters J and C we can create the mnemonic image of JUICE. Using the letters Z and S we can create the mnemonic image of the Greek god ZEUS.

07 is translated into the mnemonic letters Z J G S (0) and K C. Using the letters J and K we can create a mnemonic image of a man called JACK. Using the letters Z and K we can think of a mnemonic image of a man called ZAK.

Sensational Memory

08 is translated into the mnemonic letters Z J G S (0) and F V TH PH. Using the letters J and F we can think of a man called Jeff. Using the letters Z and PH we can create a mnemonic image of a Zephyr (a Zephyr is a classic car of which several photographs can be found on the Internet).

09 is translated into the mnemonic letters Z J G S (0) and P B. Using the letters Z and P we can create a mnemonic image of ZIP. Using the letters J and B we can create a mnemonic image of a JAB (medical syringe).

I am now going to give you a list of the alternative mnemonic letters for numbers 90 to 99 (Exercise 19). The mnemonic images may differ from your own but this will not matter so long as your images work for the purpose of recalling information:

90. PG Page (pageboy)

91. PD Pad (notepad)

92. PN Pan

93. Paw

94. PG Pig (do not confuse this with your image of a sow (6). You can distinguish the two by making one of the animals a black and pink coloured pig).

95. PL Pole (pole-vaulter).

96. B CH Beach

97. PK Pike

98. P TH Path

99. BD Bed

Exercise 20

Create another random list of 99 objects and memorise them by using the alternative mnemonic images.

Chapter 12

In this chapter we will learn and make use of another memory system. This system will interlink with the Mnemonic Alphabet system that you have just learnt. If we learn some different memory systems that interlink with each other then we have a very strong power base for a phenomenal recall.

Having learnt one memory system, we can use that system to learn another very quickly. This will enable us to go from strength to strength.

Let's examine the list of names numbered 1 to 104 on the opposite page. You will probably notice that the names are in alphabetical order in 4 columns of 26. Reading across the columns from left to right the names also appear in alphabetical order. You may also notice, looking down the list, that the names alternate male and female. All the odd numbers are male names and all the even numbers are female names.

1.	Aaron		26.	Zara
2.	Barbara		27.	Adam
3.	Callum		28.	Belinda
4.	Daisy		29.	Chris
5.	Edward		30.	Dawn
6.	Fay		31.	Edwin
7.	Gary		32.	Felicity
8.	Hannah		33.	Gerald
9.	Ian		34.	Harriet
10.	Jackie		35.	Immanuel
11.	Keith		36.	Jane
12.	Lara		37.	Ken
13.	Malcolm		38.	Linda
14.	Naomi		39.	Maurice
15.	Oliver		40.	Natalie
16.	Pamela		41.	Omar
17.	Quasimodo		42.	Pauline
18.	Rachel		43.	Quentin
19.	Samuel		44.	Rebecca
20.	Tania		45.	Simon
21.	Ulrich		46.	Theresa
22.	Valerie		47.	Ulysses
23.	Wally		48.	Vanessa
24.	Alex		49.	Wesley
25.	Yanni		50.	Roxanne

51.	Yul		76.	Trixie
52.	Zeta		77.	Johann
53.	Alan		78.	Zoe
54.	Beryl		79.	Anthony
55.	Colin		80.	Bridie
56.	Debbie		81.	Cyril
57.	Eric		82.	Deidre
58.	Fiona		83.	Ethan
59.	Graham		84.	Frances
60.	Heather		85.	Gregory
61.	Ivan		86.	Hilary
62.	Janet		87.	Ivor
63.	Kevin		88.	Julie
64.	Lorna		89.	Kirk
65.	Melvyn		90.	Lucy
66.	Nerys		91.	Michael
67.	Oscar		92.	Nina
68.	Penny		93.	Orville
69.	Quincy		94.	Petra
70.	Riana		95.	Quinn
71.	Steve		96.	Rosie
72.	Tina		97.	Stuart
73.	Uri		98.	Trudy
74.	Vera		99.	Eugene
75.	William		100.	Victoria

Remember that the human mind functions well with structure and order. We also have an innate way of responding to gender. Many of the world's languages change depending on the gender of the subject (even English to a lesser degree). This instinctive psychological detection can be used to our advantage.

This particular system is not specifically designed for memorising names and faces. We will deal with that topic in fine detail in a later chapter. However, learning this system will help you to some degree in accomplishing such tasks.

I am now going to ask you to memorise the list of 104 names and the number that they correspond to. Those names will be used as an alternative way of memorising numbers. It is not my sole intention to teach you how to memorise a series of numbers. However, if you can master the different techniques for memorising numbers you will be able to memorise all manner of things, be it text, foreign language, names and faces.

Let me give you some help on memorising the list of names. The simplest way is probably to think of people that we already know who share their name with the names on the list and tie them to the Mnemonic Alphabet images.

Unfortunately, it is difficult to find four different names for each letter. To overcome this problem I have drawn from celebrity, history and fiction.

Of course, you probably don't know 104 people who share those names. However, we live in an age where the media bombard us with names and images of celebrities. These people will suit our purpose very well. For example, I thought of the actress Catherine Zeta Jones for number 52. You may well have thought of the same person when you read the name Zeta on the list.

We can also draw from history. For example, we can create a mnemonic image for 101 on the list as Winston Churchill burning a hole in the wing of a jet (101) with his cigar.

For number 69 I thought of the actor Jack Klugman who plays Quincy in the TV series *Quincy M.E.*

Remember that, if you cannot think of a suitable image for the names on the list, you can always find information and images with an Internet search engine. As well as looking at an image, reading some biographical information on a person who is unknown to you will help to familiarise you with that individual.

When creating mnemonics we can grant ourselves a great deal of licence, so long as we are fully aware of what the image represents. For example, number 24 is represented by the name Alex. The x is so prominent in the sound of the name that it suits our purpose.

You may, if you wish, change the names to ones that you are more familiar with. However, make sure that you keep to the criteria of the names being in alphabetical order and the odd numbers being male names and even numbers being female names.

Exercise 21

Begin now to memorise the list of names in numerical order. When you have created a mnemonic image for each name and number test yourself by randomly picking numbers from a bag.

You may see items from the first list appearing involuntarily in your images. This is not necessarily a bad thing and may be helpful. However, please try to focus more on the mnemonic for the number along with the name. With a little practice the image of the person will become more prominent. When you have reached this stage, the image of the person alone will be able to represent its corresponding number.

Having completed Exercise 21, I am going to give you some additional names to add to your repertoire. We will add another five names to cover numbers 05 to 09. Remember that we will ignore the first digit (1) from 100 to 109. This is so we can create mnemonic images to represent the digits 00 to 09.

105. Anthony

106. Brenda

107. Craig

108. Dorothy

109. Errol

With a little practice, you will not need to see the Mnemonic Alphabet image to instantly recognise which number each name represents.

We now have two systems for memorising any 2-digit number from 00 to 99.

In the next chapter we will learn a final system. It is important that you master this final system thoroughly. Later you will learn how to make use of all three systems simultaneously.

Chapter 13

Exercise 22

Write a list of 109 places and locations that you are familiar with or have visited in the recent or distant past. You might find this easier by listing places in chronological order. For example, you might have childhood memories of a grandparent's home or a junior school. The further back in time you can go the better. The chronological order does not need to be precise. However, the human mind does have a sense of time, occasion and events, which we can use to our advantage.

When you write your list do not begin by numbering the locations. Write your list in vertical columns on an A4 sheet of paper. Allow spaces between each location, because you will almost certainly think of other suitable locations to fill in the spaces, as you continue with the exercise.

Performing this exercise is like going in the attic and opening a box. As you take out each item from the box more and more vivid memories will come to the fore of your mind involuntarily.

You may have initially thought that 109 places is a lot. But I can assure you that is only a minute fraction of the amount of places that your brain can recollect. Making an orderly list of this tiny fraction may take a little time, but the benefits will be more than worth the effort.

Think of 11 different places that have ten different features in each. Your list of places may look something like this:

Grandparents' home, parents' home, kindergarten, junior school, senior school, college, a vacation, workplace, current home, shopping centre and theme park.

You may have lived in different towns as a child or have worked at several different places. As a child you may have been a frequent visitor to a friend's house. If you can clearly remember 10 features in that house, garden or street then you could use someone else's home for one of your locations.

Let's take a trip around the grandparents' home to give you an idea of the type of things you can include in the list of 10 for that location.

Front garden wall

Gate

Bird table

Fishpond

Garage

Clothesline

Statue

Fireplace

Stairs

Bathroom

Once you have decided which are the most prominent features in that location, number them 1 to 10. Place a Mnemonic Alphabet image in to each of those 10 features (golf tee/tea bag, Noah's Ark, mother, door etc.).

Repeat the process for your second location. Think of 10 suitable features and number them 11 to 20. Again, use the Mnemonic Alphabet images to give each feature a numerical value.

Repeat the process with the remaining locations using the Mnemonic Alphabet images accordingly. The 10th feature of the 10th location will represent the digits 00. The 11th location and its features will represent the digits 01 to 09.

Exercise 23

Again, pick numbers randomly from a bag and recall the correct feature. When you have mastered which feature represents each of the numbers 00 to 99 then you are ready to interlink with the other systems that you have learnt in the previous chapters.

With a little practice you will not need to see the Mnemonic Alphabet image to instantly recognise which number each feature represents.

Chapter 14

Exercise 24

Memorise the following series of numbers:

1052472598461489533453786456873006580128951200356589 0
1296548

This may at first glance look like a mammoth and daunting task. However, if we size up the task in hand we can see that there are 60 digits to memorise and recall. Using the systems that we have leant we can break those 60 digits into manageable proportions.

If we use the system of food in alphabetical order (Apricot, Banana, Carrot etc.) we can break the numbers into 10 groups of 6.

By using the Location System, Name System and Mnemonic Alphabet System we can break each group of 6 numbers into 3 groups of 2.

By using the Food System we can gauge how much of the task we have accomplished. For example, in this instance, if you see

FISH in your mnemonic imagery you will know that you are halfway to completion.

The human mind likes to ask questions. By repeatedly asking three questions in a specific order, each time we see some food (from the Food System), we will be able to memorise and recall all 60 digits, in their correct sequence.

The three questions to ask are Where? (Location System) Who? (Name System) What? (Mnemonic Alphabet System). Or in other words we can think of the sequence Place Person Object.

By keeping to the order Where Who What / Place Person Object. We can simply look at one of our mnemonic scenes and quickly work out the correct sequence of numbers that it represents.

Let's create a mnemonic image for the first 6 digits of the exercise. We have established that the first mnemonic image is an APRICOT (A is the first letter of the alphabet). Imagine an apricot stuck on the prongs of a RAKE (47) by Catherine ZETA Jones (52) who is in your GRANDPARENTS' BATHROOM (10) (this was an example location that I gave you. You may have a mnemonic location of your own that you prefer to represent 10).

Reading the above paragraph the numbers appear in an incorrect order (475210) to the sequence we are memorising. However, by asking the 3 questions Where? Who? What? We can quickly recall the correct sequence:

Where? In the GRANDPARENTS' BATHROOM (10). Who? Catherine ZETA Jones (52). What? A RAKE (47). We now have the correct sequence for the first 6 digits 105247.

So you can see that we do not necessarily need to see the mnemonic image in any particular order initially. You might see the person first or the object or the location. Whichever you see first will give you a clue as to what else is in your mnemonic scene. You can simply sort out the correct sequence by answering the question Where? Who? What? in that strict order.

For good measure let's extend our Alphabetical Food System by using all 26 letters:

1. Apricot

2. Banana

3. Carrot

4. Dates

5. Egg

6. Fish

7. Grapes

8. Horseradish

9. Ice cream

10. Jelly

11. Kiwi fruit

12. Lemon

13. Melon

14. Nuts

15. Orange

16. Pear

17. Quiche

18. Raspberry

19. Strawberry

20. Tomato

21. Eucalyptus (eucalyptus can be purchased in bottles from health stores - images can be found on the internet).

22. Vinegar

23. Whisky

24. Oxtail soup

25. Yoghurt

26. Zumo (Spanish word for juice. Picture a carton of juice being poured by a Spanish Bullfighter over a Sumo wrestler - in this instance ignore the fact that we have used Sumo as a mnemonic representation of 63).

Familiarise yourself with the above list and learn the numerical value of each item. Use brand names and the commercial packaging to help you fix a clear mnemonic image in your mind.

Exercise 25

Memorise the following series of 156 numbers by using the complete Alphabetic Food System:

5489632547841236952475834912046023598024570568310457086534078953421549701243568970123468957012365014785963214501236589410321789415236856981568425785462301 71

Periodically test yourself by creating a random list of 156 numbers and memorising them using this system. By frequently performing such tests you will soon become familiar will all the mnemonic images.

Chapter 15

In this chapter we are going to create a Mnemonic Calendar. To do this we are going to create a different location system (as seen in the previous chapter).

You need to think of another 12 different locations to represent each month of the year. For each location you need to find 29 to 31 features to represent each day of the month. I advise that you include 29th February in your list.

Again, this may seem a difficult task to accomplish. However, remember that your mind has thousands upon thousands of locations and features stored away in your memory. So 366 images are a tiny fraction of what you could possibly recollect.

Your mnemonic location images need not be restricted by distance. For example, there may be several locations and features that you have not used in the surrounding area of your grandparents' home (or any of the mnemonic location images that you have formulated). They may well have lived in a distant town that has several notable features which can be used for our purpose.

Remember that you can create any journey or scene that you feel comfortable with to make up the required number of 366 days of the year. You may, if you wish, use more than one location in each month so long as you know what each image represents. There may be a neighbouring town or village that you might associate with a general area that you are thinking of.

You may not have actually visited one of these towns or villages but there could quite possibly be a church spire or prominent building that you can recollect. Such a feature can be used for our purpose.

Again, use the Mnemonic Alphabet images to help you number each day of the month. I further suggest you number each day of the year from 1 to 366. This is so that you have some more alternative images, in addition to the mnemonic number images we have learnt in previous systems, to represent those numbers. For example, to create an image of 183 using the Mnemonic Alphabet system would be quite complicated. However, your image for 1st July, which is the 183rd day of a leap year, can also be used to represent the number 183.

It is also very worthwhile extending your journey to cover numbers 1 to 999. This is an optional exercise and not necessary to master the other exercises in this book. However, if you take the time and trouble to master 999 location images you will be able to recall a 9-figure digit with just 3 images. If you have completed the previous exercises properly, you will have more than enough mental capability to memorise a series of 9 digits.

Let's look at how we might use the Mnemonic Calendar in practice. Imagine that you have a dental appointment on 3rd January. Simply picture the dentist's chair on a bird table or whatever mnemonic image you may have that represents 3rd January.

Exercise 26

Take some more small pieces of paper and number each one from 1 to 366 on one side and the corresponding date on the other. Place them in a bag. Randomly select one piece and try to correctly recall the date or number that is written on the opposite side. Repeat the exercise until you have removed each number from the bag.

Chapter 16

The following text is an extract from *The Farther Reaches Of Human Nature* by A. H. Maslow. I have chosen this extract almost completely at random. It is at first glance a complicated piece of text to memorise, especially if you have little or no knowledge of the subject to which the text is referring. It is also difficult to memorise because the text is randomly taken from the middle of a book and you have probably not got any information about the book or its author. I have deliberately chosen such text to demonstrate that it is possible to memorise virtually any written text:

3. Pluralism. The acceptance and use of individual differences in constitution and in character. Many Utopias proceeded as if all human beings were interchangeable and were equal to each other. We must accept the fact that there are very wide ranges of variation in intelligence, character, constitution, etc. Permission for individuality or the idiosyncrasy or individual freedom must specify the range of individual differences to be taken into consideration. In the fantasy Utopias there have been no feeble-minded people, no insane, no seniles, etc. Furthermore, there is frequently built in, in a covert fashion, some norm for the desirable human person, which seems to me far too narrow in view of our actual knowledge of range of variations in human beings. How fit all kinds of people into *one* set of rules or laws? Do you want to allow for a wide pluralism, e.g., of styles and fashions in clothes, shoes etc? In the United States we now permit a very wide, though not complete, range of choice among foods, but a very narrow range of choice among fashion in clothes. Fourier, for instance, founded his whole Utopian scheme in the full acceptance and use of a very wide range of constitutional differences. Plato on the other hand had only three kinds of human beings. How many kinds do you want? Can there be a society without deviants? Does the concept of self-actualisation make this question obsolete? If you accept the widest range of individual differences and the pluralism of characters and talents, then there is a society that in effect accepts much (or all) of human nature. Does self-actualisation mean in effect the acceptance of idiosyncrasy or of deviants? To what extent?

When undertaking having to memorise a section of text as above, the first thing to do is count the number of sentences of text there are in total. In this instance there are 17 sentences so the Food Alphabet system can be comfortably employed for this task.

Let's have a look at how we might memorise the first sentence:

3.Pluralism. The acceptance and use of individual differences in constitution and in character.

We can picture a mnemonic image of a mother that represents the number 3 eating several apricots. An image of multiple apricots represents the word pluralism. In the English language most plural words end with the letter S. To reinforce your mnemonic see the apricots that are about to be eaten laid out in an S-shape. Imagine that the apricots that the mother is about to eat are in a field that is being ploughed. The word plough will indicate a clue as to the sound of pluralism. Extending this a little further you may want to reflect on the word rural. This is because a plough can be easily associated with a rural scene and the sound rural rhymes with plural.

Somewhere near the S-shaped line of apricots I picture John Travolta in his classic *Saturday Night Fever* pose (an Internet search will give you several images) brandishing an axe in his raised hand and a sceptre, performing a dance having just chopped off the hand of an Arab called Yousef.

Let's look at the keywords that have been used in the above paragraph: Axe Sceptre Dance Hand Yousef. If you read those words quickly they sound like "acceptance and use of."

We can easily associate John Travolta with dancing but seeing him brandishing an axe with a sceptre is quite bizarre and raises our attention. We can associate an axe with a gruesome act such as chopping off someone's hand. We can identify chopping off someone's hand as a form of traditional Arabic punishment. We can associate the Yousef as coming from the Middle East or Arabia.

Continuing, I picture a Hindi (Indian wearing a turban). Here I think of another association of Eastern religion and think of the word Veda (any or all of the most ancient sacred writings of Hinduism). Please note how I have drawn on associations even though they may be a little tenuous. In the background I visualise two men standing back to back, each holding a gun as if in a duel.

The keywords from above are Hindi Veda Duel, which gives us the sound of "individual". You may wish to replace the word

Sensational Memory

Veda with an image of a video. I have deliberately used the word Veda as an example of how to draw on association. A video probably makes a much better mnemonic, as it is a tangible and visual object.

Surprisingly, I place the above images in the location I have for 2nd July along with an image of a tiny wren carrying a pair of scissors. I see the scissors cut into the White House where there is an actor in front of a theatrical mirror (mirror surrounded by light bulbs) putting on makeup with his hand.

You may well ask why have I used an image of 2nd July? My reasoning may not seem straightforward but it is effective. The 2nd July is the 184th day of the year. If we transpose 184 into the Mnemonic Alphabet we will have the letters DFR and by seeing a tiny wren with a pair scissors, we will have a mnemonic image to represent the word differences (DFR Wren Scissors). Incidentally, my image for 2nd July is a model railway that I once visited.

The image of the White House represents the word constitution. Again an image of a hand represents the word "and". The image of an actor putting on makeup represents the words "in character" (actors get "in character" to play their roles by putting on makeup).

Replace the light bulbs around the theatrical mirror with apricots to signify that you have completed a mnemonic image for the first piece of text. You can also place a small cross in each of the apricots. The cross will represent 13 (tomb) the number of words included in the mnemonic image. Taking stock of the number of words that you are required to memorise will give you a sense of control and build your confidence.

I should point out that this final mnemonic image is only there as an approximate guide. It is not totally necessary to create mnemonic images for every preposition in every sentence (in, at, to etc.). If you memorise the keywords through mnemonic imagery your subconscious mind will be able to find the correct prepositions naturally to reconstruct a sentence.

There is something else we can do with the image. You may have noticed that the text we are memorising is written in italics (as in the original book). In this instance, we can tilt the image 45 degrees as if looking at a badly adjusted TV screen image. Taking such action causes us to peer more closely at the image. The slanting image helps make our images appear more interesting. Gaining and maintaining interest is very important to keeping our memory enthused and energized.

These images may take a little bit of time and effort to formulate but with practice you will be able to create them with speed and efficiency.

Exercise 27

Recall the images that have been created and translate them back into the text. As you see the text state the words out loud. Repeat the exercise several times until you can state the text fluently and with ease.

Stating text out loud has at least two benefits:

1. Spoken words are filtered into the mind's memory and enhance your power of recall.

2. Repeatedly speaking the same words enhances facial muscle memory.

Initially this is not an easy exercise. Please try to maintain a confident belief in your ability. Keeping calm and relaxed is conducive to your recall working efficiently. It is a common occurrence that someone might misplace a set of keys and search without success. However, it is when they stop looking and do something else, that suddenly the image of where they left the keys involuntarily springs to mind. The required information comes to the fore of their mind because they are relaxed.

Don't be afraid to readjust your mnemonic images to suit you. Compact and embroider your images so that you don't have to search too hard for important key mnemonics.

To be frank, my mind went blank when I first tried to recall the text. I got as far as *3. Pluralism* and I could not progress. I could only remember a number and one word at the beginning of a piece text consisting of 13 words.

It is not uncommon for the human mind to have a blank moment. But we have the skill and ingenuity to overcome such problems that occur from time to time. With practice, solving such problems will become as simple as changing a light bulb! There is no need to sit helplessly in the dark.

So how did I solve my problem? Firstly, I relaxed and gently reflected on what images and feelings I could muster from my mnemonic scene without feeling anxious. I was able to sense somewhere near the beginning of the mnemonic that there was some sort of movement. The sensation of movement led me to the word "dance". The word "dance" conjured the image of people dancing holding credit cards in their hands. Originally I thought about credit cards to represent the word "accept".

Shops often have signs stating that they "Accept" credit cards. Unfortunately, this image did not work, as it was too obscure

Recognising that I had a weakness in my mnemonic imagery I took measures to strengthen it. In this instance, I pictured John Travolta in his classic *Saturday Night Fever* pose and placed him in the ploughed field amongst the apricots that are lined up in an S-shape.

Remember that by drawing on existing images and placing them into a new scene will enhance your power of recall. I had originally made a mistake by not making my image specific enough. To think of someone dancing is somewhat vague as opposed to picturing an iconic figure such as John Travolta.

As human beings we are prone to making mistakes. As you develop your mnemonic skills you will be able to recognise and understand how and why you have made the occasional mistake. Your understanding will lead you to a solution that will suit your purpose. You will see these problems as challenges and will gain great satisfaction as you overcome them. When it comes to mnemonics I think of the Sandie Shaw song, *There's always something there to remind me*. With practice you will learn that those words are so true.

You may have some concern about comprehension of the text that you are memorising. After all, the mnemonic images are bizarre and bare little or no resemblance to the text in normal everyday language. However, you will be pleased to learn that soon after your mnemonic images have filtered into your mind and you are able to express those images as normal word for word language, your subconscious mind will begin to comprehend the new information, as intended by its original author.

Learning to use mnemonics is like riding a bicycle. It is quicker by foot to make a short journey if you have not learnt how to ride a bicycle. However, if you manage to overcome the problem of balancing a bicycle in motion, you will be able to make several more journeys and cover more distance at a much greater speed by bicycle, with only a fraction of the effort of walking.

Learning to ride a bicycle takes some considerable courage. However, little courage is required once you have mastered the art. It takes time, practice and the courage to fail before you consistently succeed.

2nd Sentence:

"Many Utopias proceeded as if all human beings were interchangeable and were equal to each other."

To explain how I memorised this sentence I am going to describe my mnemonic scene and explain the whys and wherefores afterwards, although some of it will be apparent without any explanation:

I picture bananas floating in the sea and amongst them is a German U-boat towing a charity box that is covered in seeds, underneath two piers. On one of the piers I picture an Asian man called Asif who is hauling in a human skull that is full of beans from the sea.

Again, on the pier I see a werewolf go into the slot machine arcade towards the booth where change is given. Standing near the booth is a bull. Suddenly another werewolf jumps on the bull's back and knocks off two stacks of coins, with an eagle sitting on each stack, tossing coins to each other.

At first glance you may think that I have omitted to make a mnemonic for the word "many". However, as I have described a German U-boat, it is easy to make an association with the word Germany that does in fact contain the letters m a n y. It is often a good idea to think how words, sounds and images might be spelt. By doing this we can frequently grasp useful information.

In addition, you could picture a Swastika flag that is torn in half to prompt you to think of half the letters of Germany to give you the word "many". The word "many" will appear frequently in several texts. The half Swastika flag can be added to your Mnemonic Vocabulary to represent the word "many" in future.

You will soon find yourself being able to create symbols that you can use time and time again. Mnemonics is a language in itself.

The letter U is the most prominent letter in the word U-boat and is also the most prominent letter in the word Utopia. Since a U-boat is a nautical vessel it is easy to make an association with the word towing. As we are now going to create a nautical scene, a pier would not be incongruous. In this instance I have imagined two piers to signify pluralism (i.e. Utopias).

The charity box represents the word proceeds as the proceeds go to charity. The image of the seeds gives a clue to the latter part of the word "proceeds".

The name Asif is a popular Asian name that serves the purpose of representing the words "as if". Seeing Asif hauling represents the word "all". Try to see him struggling and straining with a fishing line. This again would be in keeping with our nautical scene.

When visualising actions like towing and hauling think about the way they are spelt as you create the mnemonic and make a mental note to ignore the letters ing.

The human skull represents the word "human" and the beans represent the word "beings".

The werewolf represents the word "were". Seeing the werewolf "running into" hints at the word "inter". The slot machine arcade is a place where you would expect to see a booth for change. You have already accepted that "a bull" sounds like "able". The words "into change bull" will quickly give us the word "interchangeable".

The second werewolf must come into the scene as soon as you see the bull. The second werewolf represents the second "were". Coins are often stacked in piles of equal height. An eagle sounds like equal and their interaction with the coins will give a hint to the words "to each other".

At the end of the mnemonic image I place some bananas in a dish (16) to signify that I have covered all 16 words in the second sentence.

Exercise 28

Recall the images that have been created and translate them back into the text. As you see the text state the words out loud. Repeat the exercise several times until you can state the text fluently and with ease.

Exercise 29

Recite all the text you have memorised thus far.

3rd Sentence:

"We must accept the fact that there are very wide ranges of variation in intelligence, character, constitution, etc."

To explain how I memorised this sentence I am going to describe my mnemonic scene and explain the whys and wherefores afterwards, although some of it will be apparent without any explanation:

I picture a carrot being eaten by a Frenchman wearing a Breton shirt and a beret, with a moustache dripping with French mustard. He is nodding his head as if in agreement with something. In his right hand he is brandishing an axe and holding a sceptre in the other.

In the background there is a derelict factory and I can just about see the former British Prime Minister Mrs Thatcher who pushes a fairy out of a wide-open window on to the firing ranges. The fairy jumps on the back of half a Dalmatian dog which chases Brains, a character from *Thunderbirds*, into the White House where Yul Brynner is waiting.

At the end of the mnemonic image I dip some carrots in toffee (18) to signify that I have covered all 18 words in the third sentence.

Let's examine my mnemonic imagery more closely and see how it serves my purpose:

The carrot as you know signifies the 3rd line or sentence in the text. In Western culture a nodding head signifies the word "Yes". If a Frenchman nods his head he is probably thinking *Oui*, which is pronounced as "We". The moustache with the dripping French mustard gives us the word "must". You could just focus on the moustache but the French mustard compounds the mnemonic. An iconic image of a Frenchman usually has a moustache and could be easily mistaken as insignificant. The French mustard draws more attention to it.

The above creates a mnemonic for the words "We must".

The axe and sceptre are employed again to represent the word "accept". Notice how I deliberately place the axe in the right hand and the sceptre in the left. As I look at the mnemonic image I see the axe to my left and the sceptre to my right. In Western culture we read text from left to right and that is how I view the axe and sceptre to sense the cues in the correct order.

The derelict factory and the only partly visible Mrs Thatcher gives us "the fact that". This is similar to the technique used in the 2nd line of seeing just half a Swastika to represent the word "many".

A fairy sounds like "very" and a fairy being pushed through a wide-open window gives us the words "very wide". The firing ranges automatically gives us the word "ranges".

A fairy on the back of a half Dalmatian gives us "variation". The puppet, Brains, gives us the word "intelligence" as brains are associated with intelligence. Brains is, as I am sure you know, a character from the popular TV series *Thunderbirds* thus giving us the word "character".

Again an image of the White House represents the word "constitution". The image of Yul Brynner represents "etc." This is because in the film *The King and I* the character played by Yul Brynner famously delivered the line, "Etc. etc. etc."

Exercise 30

Recall the images that have been created and translate them back into the text. As you see the text state the words out loud. Repeat the exercise several times until you can state the text fluently and with ease.

Exercise 31

Recite all the text you have memorised thus far.

4th Sentence:

"Permission for individuality or the idiosyncrasy or individual freedom must specify the range of individual differences to be taken into consideration."

The mnemonic scene:

I stick (although this word sounds ugly there is an association between a date and stickiness) a date on a parking permit and place it on the exhaust pipe of my car. On the door of my car (almost causing a strain on the hinges) is a Hindi drinking a cup of tea. In the next parking space there are 4 oars laid in a square. In the square is a jester (village idiot) sitting in a bathroom sink.

He also has an oar and strikes a woman called Freda with this oar, who is wearing a turban and sucking a dummy. She removes her dummy, dips it in mustard and places it in the centre of a target on a firing range. Behind the target are two Hindis standing back to back, each holding a pistol, and as they stride away in opposite directions a model train passes between them. After the train passes, two bees carrying a token fly into a Gypsy fortune-teller's tent. At the entrance of the tent is a mosquito net full of dates.

Explanation:

The date represents the 4th sentence of the text. The word "permission" stems from the noun "permit". My subconscious came up with parking permit partly because there is alliteration with the letter P. Initial images are usually the best to work with (first impressions last). So I had decided I would set my scene in a car park that I am familiar with.

I place the parking permit on my car's exhaust pipe. There has been a great deal of political discussion about car emissions in recent years. So by placing a permit on the exhaust pipe I was able to create a mnemonic for "permission".

The image of the car door represents the word "for" (sounds like "four"). Although I have mentioned that it is not always necessary to have mnemonic images for prepositions such as: as, at, for, in, on etc, I will create one if one comes to mind without too much time and effort.

The mnemonic image of a Hindi or simply a turban will pertain to the word "individual". In this instance, the Hindi is drinking a cup of tea (Indian tea to reinforce the mnemonic) and the image as a whole will represent "individuality". Because I have established that a Hindi is going to pertain to the word "individual" it is not necessary to have a mnemonic for each syllable.

The four oars in a square will represent the words "for or". The image of a square can be used to represent for or four. Remember the human mind likes to deal with geometric shapes. In everyday speech we do have an expression "four square" and such an image will suit our purpose.

A square is also useful as we can place another image inside it almost like a picture frame. We can see the four-sided frame and ask, 'What's inside the frame?'

In this instance, inside the frame of four oars was the mnemonic image of a jester or village idiot with a bathroom sink that gave me the word "idiosyncrasy" (although a jester and a village idiot are not quite the same thing they are similar enough to serve my need). There is no need to find a mnemonic image for the letters "crasy" although you could think of a jester as having "crazy" antics.

I pictured Freda Payne (singer who had a hit recording *Band of Gold*) sucking a dummy. Of course, if I knew someone personally called Freda I could have used their image. I was familiar with the name of Freda Payne and an Internet search gave me several images of the celebrity.

The mnemonic image of the dummy gave me the sound of "dom" in the word "freedom". Seeing Freda with a dummy whilst wearing a turban (Hindi) gave me the words, "individual freedom".

The mustard again gives me the word "must" and seeing the dummy with mustard being placed in the centre of a target on a firing range gives me the words "must specify the range".

We have already created a mnemonic image of a firing range and having established this image we can use it again as that image is now familiar to us. Remember, placing new information with established information makes new information memorable.

In everyday language we hear of people talking about specific targets. An image of a target can be representative of the word "specify". Targets are found on a firing range so this mnemonic scene will give us the words "specify the range".

The two Hindis standing back to back, each holding a pistol gives me the word "individual". Although we have discussed an image of a Hindi or a turban as representing something pertaining to the word "individual", I have created an image of a duel to enable me to create some form of action and drama in the mnemonic scene. In this instance I see the two Hindis walking in opposite directions (as if they have a difference of opinion) and see a model train passing between them. You may recall that a model train represents the 2nd July, which is the 184th day of a leap year, and the mnemonic letters for 184 are DFR. The letters DFR again give me a cue for the word "differences".

Having seen the train pass I see two bees carrying a token. This image represents "to be taken". With a little imagination you could picture two bees carrying a token that is something similar to what you might put in a slot machine. The two bees obviously represent the words "to be". You may already be familiar with a token that you use regularly. You can use this as a standard mnemonic image to represent the word "taken" in future.

Seeing the two bees flying inside something will hint at the word "into". In this instance the two bees fly into a Gypsy fortune-teller's tent. The Gypsy fortune-teller's tent, somewhat bizarrely, gives me the word "consideration". For this I drew upon a little unusual but pre-existing knowledge that I had obtained from an interest I had in astrology. The word "consider" literally means "to be with the stars" or "to consult the stars". The Latin word for stars is *sidus*.

Drawing on snippets of unusual pieces of information makes good anchors for mnemonics.

If and when you come across a word that you have difficulty in creating a representative mnemonic image for, try to break the word down into small syllabic components and try to find images that you can meld to make one word. We have seen examples of this in the words "variation" (fairy and Dalmatian), and "permission" (permit and emission).

Another good idea is to consult a dictionary and read about its definition and etymology to give you fresh ideas.

Finally, to close the fourth sentence I picture a net (a mosquito net is easily associated with a tent), which is covered with dates. This image indicates that there are approximately 21 words represented in the mnemonic image.

Exercise 32

Recall the images that have been created and translate them back into the text. As you see the text state the words out loud. Repeat the exercise several times until you can state the text fluently and with ease.

Exercise 33

Recite all the text you have memorised thus far.

5th Sentence:

"In the fantasy Utopias there have been no feeble-minded people, no insane, no seniles, etc."

The mnemonic scene:

I picture someone throwing eggs against an inn sign. The inn is on a cliff overlooking the sea. In the sea are cans of *Fanta* floating in the water amongst which two U-boats appear. Between the U-boats a large map is unscrolled revealing a huge half bean from which Ursula Andress appears wearing a snorkel and mask. She throws the snorkel and mask at a miner and knocks his helmet off. The miner is accompanying a bull kneeling on all fours. The bull also has a ticket that says "no charge".

The bull looks through a kaleidoscope and sees the Eiffel Tower. From the Eiffel Tower there are some elderly people with Zimmer frames jumping into the River Seine. In the river there are some sea lions whose bodies are spirally twisted swimming around Yul Brynner who has a dish of eggs on his head.

Explanation:

The eggs represent the fifth sentence. The image of the inn gives me the word "in". The image of a cliff has no particular significance other than drawing my attention to the inn and sea. Seeing cans of *Fanta* (well-known soft drink) gives me the word "fantasy" and the two U-boats gives me the word "Utopias". In this instance I have pictured two U-boats to signify pluralism (i.e. Utopias).

The map represents the word "there". As you can imagine, it is virtually impossible to think of an immediate mnemonic image for a word such as "there" so I have chosen something that refers to location. In this instance a map suits the purpose. When memorising text, the word "there" appears frequently and to have a mnemonic image such as a map will prove very useful.

So add the image of a map to represent the word "there" to your Mnemonic Vocabulary.

The half bean represents the words "have been" and Ursula Andress, who is the actress who played the Bond girl in the film *Dr No*, will be representative of the word "no". For this image I picture Ursula Andress carrying a snorkel and mask (images of Ursula Andress as the Bond girl can be found on the Internet). You may, if you wish, in future just picture a snorkel and mask to represent the word "no".

The bull with the ticket stating "no charge" represents the word "feeble" (fee - bull). The fact that the bull is kneeling on all fours signifies that the bull is stationary and not charging.

The word "charge" is a synonym of the word "fee" and to strengthen the mnemonic we can make a quick association with the word "charge" and a bull.

The word "miner" is used because it sounds like "minded" and having established a mnemonic word for feeble, our mind naturally leads to the words feeble-minded.

A kaleidoscope is another word that can be added to your Mnemonic Vocabulary to represent the word "people". This is because a kaleidoscope has a peephole, which sounds like "people". Although you could picture people to represent the word "people", this may well cause confusion as various people are used in our mnemonic images. Having such an unusual singular object such as a kaleidoscope makes our task much easier. A kaleidoscope makes a useful and versatile mnemonic tool as it lends itself to see different images.

The mnemonic image of a bull can be used frequently as the letters "ble" are a common suffix. To strengthen the mnemonic we can also think of the words "bull's-eye". Again, an eye lends itself for looking at new images.

I picture the Eiffel Tower because it stands near the River Seine and to see people jumping in the River Seine gives us the word "insane".

The Zimmer frames signify elderly people which is tenuous with senility. Because this is a very weak link I have created a mnemonic image of twisted sea lions. The twisted sea lions is a spoonerism of "seniles". Try to picture the actual bodies of the sea lions as spirally twisted, almost like a twisted length of rope. In this instance the twist signifies that there is a change in the permutation of the phonetic sound.

Again, the image of Yul Brynner represents "etc."

Finally to signify that there are 16 words in the fifth sentence picture a dish holding some eggs balanced on Yul Brynner's bald head.

Exercise 34

Recall the images that have been created and translate them back into the text. As you see the text state the words out loud. Repeat the exercise several times until you can state the text fluently and with ease.

Exercise 35

Recite all the text you have memorised thus far.

6th Sentence:

"Furthermore, there is frequently built in, in a covert fashion, some norm for the desirable human person, which seems to me far too narrow in view of our actual knowledge of range of variations in human beings."

The mnemonic scene:

I picture a father figure dangling a fish over the fictional character Oliver Twist, who passes a map to Quasimodo who is driving a Bentley. On his hump is a parrot with its bill in a tin. The parrot throws the tin at the Olympic runner Sebastian Coe who is carrying a cushion with a green Swastika. He throws the cushion at a Norman soldier who is holding a calculator, which is displaying the number four. In the background there are two cannibals sat at a table, on a desert island, amongst the rubble, licking their lips, as they are about to have lunch. On the table is a steaming human body holding a purse.

Above them flies a witch wearing a split skirt with a lump of coal whilst carrying a tome. She flies over a bridge. Passing under the bridge are two narrow barges with a Frenchman looking through binoculars. He sees an hourglass. Inside the hourglass is a hacksaw sawing into a jewel. Behind the hourglass is an owl hovering over a firing range. A fairy riding two Dalmatians runs across the range amongst some human skulls and beans. Finally I see a fish in a microphone stand.

Explanation:

The fish represents the 6th sentence. The father figure (an image of your own father or maybe a priest) represents the word "Further" as they sound similar. The fictional character Oliver Twist was known as "the boy who asked for more" and consequently represents the word "more". The mnemonic image of a map again gives us the word "there". The fictional character Quasimodo had the misfortune of being considered a freak. But to see him in a Bentley will give us the word "frequently". Since Quasimodo was known as "The Hunchback of Notre Dame" I naturally look to place something on his hump. In this instance I placed a parrot. We can easily associate a parrot sitting on a pirate's shoulder. To see a parrot on a hunched back is not too dissimilar.

Picturing a parrot with its bill in a tin represents the words "built in". The image of Sebastian Coe gives me the first syllable of "covert". The colour green gives me the second syllable "vert". This is because the word *vert* is French for green. The Swastika gives me the first syllable of "fashion" (Fascism) and the cushion gives me the second syllable. Consequently, I have a mnemonic image for the words "covert fashion."

I should point out that although we used a mnemonic image of Quasimodo and a tin in this instance, these images do not represent numbers. You may recall that Quasimodo from the Mnemonic Names list represents 17 and a tin from the Mnemonic Alphabet list represents 12. It is perfectly acceptable to use pre-existing mnemonic images to represent something entirely different, so long as we are clear as to what they represent in any given instance.

The image of a Norman soldier holding a calculator gives us the words "some norm". The Norman soldier represents the word "norm". The Normans had a very distinctive uniform, particularly their helmets and chain mail.

It is difficult to think of an immediate mnemonic image for the word "some". But a calculator is an instrument for calculating a sum, which sounds like "some". The word "some" is quite commonly used in written text so a mnemonic image of a calculator is worth adding to your Mnemonic Vocabulary. Calculators display numbers so I make use of this characteristic and see a number 4 to represent the word "for".

Although the two mnemonic images for the words "some norm for" do not appear in sequence this will not cause a problem. The subconscious mind will automatically figure out the correct order. In a similar manner, the subconscious mind has the ability to read words upside down, back to front and sideways effortlessly.

The image of the cannibals licking their lips gives me the words "desirable human person". The reason for this image may be somewhat obscure so I add to the mnemonic image to give clues as to what sounds I need to recollect. It is easy to associate cannibals as being on a desert island. We can also associate a desert island as having some ancient stones and ruins (e.g. Easter Island - see images on the Internet). Some of these stones could be just lying as rubble. If we take the first syllables of "desert island" then add them to the word "rubble", we will have the sound "desirable".

The image of the steaming human body holding a purse gives me the words "human person". The steam has no real significance, other than to indicate that the human body has been prepared as a meal for the two cannibals, who might think of what is served in front of them as "desirable".

The image of a witch wearing a split skirt with a piece of coal gives me the words "which seems". The split in the skirt could be a tear in the seam. The piece of coal again indicates to the sound of seam (coal seam - seem).

Again the word "seem" is quite commonly used in written text so a mnemonic image of a piece of coal to represent "seem" is worth adding to your Mnemonic Vocabulary.

A tome is a very large book and could be associated with a witch's book of spells. The mnemonic image of a tome gives us the words "to me".

The bridge gives me the word "far". I have taken this from the film title *A Bridge Too Far*. Although to date I have not seen the film, my scant knowledge is enough for me to create a mnemonic image for the word "far". It is not necessary to have in-depth knowledge of the things we use for mnemonics. So long as the snippets of information are steadfast in our psyche then we can anchor things to them.

If I use a bridge as a mnemonic I will look to see if there is something crossing over it or something passing under it. This will give me a natural link to the next mnemonic. So when you use a bridge in your mnemonic image remember to think of "over and under".

The two narrow barges will give us the words "too narrow". A pair of binoculars can easily be associated with the word " view". However, by using a Frenchman holding the binoculars, the common French word *vous* springs to mind and reinforces the mnemonic.

The hourglass represents the word "our". This is another useful mnemonic image to add to your vocabulary. The fact that an hourglass is transparent enables us to imagine other images inside it or through it in the background

We can easily imagine a hacksaw cutting into a jewel to give us the word "actual". The mnemonic image of an owl gives the word "knowledge". An owl is associated with the word wise (e.g. "He is a wise old owl"). Wisdom can pertain to knowledge and the word "knowledge" contains the letters "OWL" in that sequence.

With a little imagination we can see such a bird of prey hovering to give us the word "of". Again the mnemonic imagine of a firing range gives us the word "range". The fairy riding the two Dalmatians gives us the word "variations". The human skulls and beans give us the words "human beings".

The fish in the microphone stand informs us that there were approximately 37 words to recall in the 6th sentence.

Exercise 36

Recall the images that have been created and translate them back into the text. As you see the text state the words out loud. Repeat the exercise several times until you can state the text fluently and with ease.

Exercise 37

Recite all the text you have memorised thus far.

7th Sentence:

"How fit all kinds of people into *one* set of rules or laws?"

(To be frank, I found the structure of this sentence a little odd, however, this is how it is printed in the original text.)

The mnemonic scene:

I see a Red Indian chief with a bunch of grapes in his headdress. He is holding up his right hand as if greeting someone. In his left hand he is holding a dumb-bell whilst raising and lowering his arm continuously.

Whilst the Red Indian chief is doing his exercises a young girl, who is sat on a settee, is mending one of his socks. Also sat on the settee are a Negro, a Jew, an Arab and a Chinaman each holding a kaleidoscope. Behind them is a judge holding a ruler measuring a badger.

Finally, I see a bunch of grapes on a cross.

Explanation:

The grapes represent the 7th sentence. The Red Indian chief holding up his right hand, as if greeting someone, represents the word "how" (traditional Red Indian greeting). The dumb-bell and exercise represents the word "fit".

The young girl mending a sock needs a little further explanation as its meaning is not immediate. The process of mending a sock is called darning. Someone who darns could be described as a darner. This gives me the girl's name Dana. However, in 1970 there was a young girl singer called Dana who had a number 1 hit with a song called *All Kinds of Everything* (this song is easily accessible on the Internet). This image gives me the words "all kinds of".

Although this mnemonic is not straightforward and somewhat subjective it is, for me, highly effective for the purpose. I am certain that when you begin to create mnemonics for yourself, you will automatically draw from your personal experiences and knowledge. One of the fascinating things about creating mnemonics is that it draws out information and memories from within you that you thought you might have forgotten. You may have experienced this whilst creating your mnemonic list of places and locations.

The settee indicates to the word "set". Also a settee is a piece of furniture that is designed for seating more than one person, so having seen a settee I naturally look for more than one person. In this instance there are some people of different creeds and colours each holding a kaleidoscope (peephole - people, as discussed earlier). This image reinforces the words "all kinds of people".

The judge with ruler represents the words "rules and laws". The badger represents the word "set" as a badger's habitat is called a set. Although I have used a settee to represent the word "set", the image of such a piece or furniture may be a little ambiguous as it could also be described as a sofa or a couch.

The grapes represent the 6th sentence and the cross (tomb) represents that there are approximately 13 words in the sentence.

Exercise 38

Recall the images that have been created and translate them back into the text. As you see the text state the words out loud. Repeat the exercise several times until you can state the text fluently and with ease.

Exercise 39

Recite all the text you have memorised thus far.

8th Sentence

"Do you want to allow for a wide pluralism, e.g., of styles and fashions in clothes, shoes etc?"

Mnemonic scene:

I picture the Swedish pop group Abba and blond-haired sixties pop star Adam Faith on stage covered in horseradish.

I see Adam Faith holding up a megaphone calling through a wide-open window that overlooks two ploughs in a field. In the field there is a broken egg on a stile. On the other side of the stile is a cushion with a Swastika and some shoes on a rotary clothesline, which is being spun round by Yul Brynner.

Finally, I see some toffees in horseradish.

Explanation:

The horseradish represents the 8th sentence. The Swedish group Abba had a hit record called *Voulez-Vous*. and *Voulez-vous* is French for "do you want". However, Abba had many hits and I need a mnemonic to specify which particular hit recording I am trying to recollect. In this instance I picture the sixties pop singer Adam Faith who had a hit record called *What Do You Want?*. Although Adam Faith had several other hits, placing him amongst the Swedish pop group Abba can only indicate to the one theme they had in common, in this instance the words "do you want".

A megaphone is an apparatus used for calling aloud. However, the word "aloud" can be spelt as "allowed" which pertains to "allow". A megaphone makes a useful mnemonic for words pertaining to "allow" so it is useful to add this image to your Mnemonic Vocabulary.

We have already discussed the use of a window to represent the word "wide" in a previous line. We have also already created a mnemonic for the word "pluralism" at the beginning of the chapter.

The broken egg represents "e.g." (common abbreviation meaning "for example"). The brokenness represents the fact that the egg is not complete or in this instance I am trying to recollect the letters e g. This image of a broken egg can be added to your Mnemonic Vocabulary.

A stile fits into our rural image but more importantly sounds like "style (s)". The cushion with the Swastika, as we have already discussed, represents "fashion (s)" I have deliberately used a rotary clothesline because this facilitates action in the mnemonic image. I do not simply use an image of clothes, as this could be a little nebulous. When you see a clothesline you subconsciously hear the word "clothes". If you were simply just to imagine clothes, you might think of garments, socks, shirts trousers etc. and not specifically the word "clothes".

The image of the shoes on a clothesline is prominent enough to be self-explanatory. And as previously discussed, the mnemonic image of Yul Brynner gives us the word "etc."

The horseradish represents the 8th sentence and the toffee represents that there are approximately 18 words to recall.

Exercise 40

Recall the images that have been created and translate them back into the text. As you see the text state the words out loud. Repeat the exercise several times until you can state the text fluently and with ease.

Exercise 41

Recite all the text you have memorised thus far.

9th Sentence:

"In the United States we now permit a very wide, though not complete, range of choice among foods, but a very narrow range of choice among fashion in clothes."

The mnemonic scene:

I picture the Statue of Liberty holding a giant ice cream. On the balcony is a French man nodding his head whilst holding a stopwatch in one hand and a Kermit the Frog puppet, which has a passport in its mouth, in the other. He partly opens a window to allow a fairy to fly out. The fairy flies across a firing range. On the firing range there is a monk who has eaten half a choc-ice and is surrounded by various fruit, vegetables and meats. There is also a very large pack of butter that has melted to form a lake. Floating on the lake is a narrow barge with a firing range target. By the target there is another monk eating another choc-ice whilst turning a rotary clothesline from which hangs a cushion with a Swastika.

Finally, I see some ice cream melting in a nappy.

Explanation:

The Statue of Liberty represents "In the United States". The giant ice cream represents that it is the 9th sentence. The French man nodding his head represents the word "we" as discussed previously. The stopwatch represents the word "now". This image can be added to your Mnemonic Vocabulary as the word "now" appears frequently in text.

The image of Kermit the Frog holding a passport gives me the word "permit". Kermit rhymes with the word "permit" and the passport is a kind of permit. By using a passport we also have alliteration with the letter P.

As already discussed, a window represents the word "wide". Also as discussed, a fairy represents the word "very". In this instance the window is only partly open and this image will give us the words "though not complete".

As discussed, a firing range represents the word "range". The monk represents the word "among". This image should also be added to your Mnemonic Vocabulary because words like "among" and "amongst" appear frequently in printed text.

You probably will have noticed that many of the mnemonic images are recurring. This is quite often the case when trying to memorise a piece of text on a given subject. This means that our task becomes a little easier as we are able to draw from our Mnemonic Vocabulary.

The half-eaten choc-ice represents the word "choice". This is simply because the word contains almost exactly the same letters for the word "choice" in the correct sequence. This is another useful image to be added to your Mnemonic Vocabulary.

The image of fruit, vegetables and meats gives me the word "foods". This is simply because fruit, vegetables and meats more or less covers foods in general.

The image of butter gives me the word "but". This is another common word and butter should be added to your Mnemonic Vocabulary.

The image of a narrow barge, as already discussed, gives me the word "narrow". I deliberately melted the butter to create a lake so I could accommodate an image of a narrow barge with ease.

All the remaining mnemonic images for this sentence have been discussed previously.

The ice cream melting in the nappy tells me that there are approximately 29 words in the 9th sentence.

Exercise 42

Recall the images that have been created and translate them back into the text. As you see the text state the words out loud. Repeat the exercise several times until you can state the text fluently and with ease.

Exercise 43

Recite all the text you have memorised thus far.

10th Sentence:

"Fourier, for instance, founded his whole Utopian scheme in the full acceptance and use of a very wide range of constitutional differences."

The mnemonic scene:

I see a Gypsy eating a wobbly jelly. He is wearing an earring that is shaped like a number 4. The earring falls into a jar of instant coffee. The jar is standing inside the white line that marked where a dead body had lain on the green of a golf course. Adjacent to the green is a lake from which emerges a U-boat towing a water skier who has a large yellow M on his wetsuit

Chris Hare

On the other side of the lake John Travolta brandishing an axe and sceptre sits in an overflowing steaming bath. An Arab is washing his back and a fairy opens a window that overlooks a driving range. Golf balls are seen flying towards the White House, which has a model railway running around its balcony.

Finally, I see a nun eating a jelly.

Explanation:

The jelly represents the 10th sentence. Please note that I have described the jelly as a wobbly jelly as jelly has a propensity to wobble. Also this gives me a chance to include some action in the imagery. As previously discussed, movement and action are powerful tools to be used in mnemonics.

The Gypsy with the earring shaped like a number four gives me the name "Fourier". The reason I pictured a Gypsy is because Gypsies traditionally wear earrings and I needed something that sounded familiar to ear to give the second syllable of the name.

The four-shaped earring falling in the instant coffee jar gave me the words "for instance". When you read the original text out loud, continue to see the images as you speak. You will be able to recall the text more and more fluently but some of the images will remain as cues should you stumble.

The white line outlining where a dead body lay gives me the word "founded" as it sounds like "found dead". Such lines are often seen in police detective and murder mystery TV programmes.

The image of a golf green gives me the word "whole" which sounds like "hole". It is generally known that the object of the game of golf is to place a ball in a hole. The iconic image of a flag in a golf hole will prove very useful in representing the word "whole".

Should you create a mnemonic scene, such as golf course, it is worthwhile looking at what other typical features could be associated with that scene. In this instance, I made use of the fact that golf courses often have a lake as a feature.

The lake easily lends itself to place an image of a U-boat which, as already discussed, is a mnemonic representing the word "Utopia" or in this particular sentence "Utopian". It is not always necessary to create two mnemonic images to differentiate between similar words. However, I could be pedantic and include an image of someone called Ian to give me "Utopian". The letters "ian" are a common suffix and an image of someone called Ian will prove useful in future.

I think of the large letter M logo of the famous fast food chain *McDonald's*. It is easy to imagine the water-skier wearing the logo as part of a sponsorship contract. The image of the skier and the large letter M gives me the word "scheme".

If you create a mnemonic image of a lake it is again worthwhile looking at what other typical features could be associated with that scene. For instance all lakes have a shoreline, which can be used as a reference point to look at for the next mnemonic image.

The mnemonic images of John Travolta, an Arab (Yousef), a fairy and a window have been used previously. The steaming, overflowing bath gives me the word "full". The steam is only bought into the mnemonic to add a little action and drama to the scene.

In this instance, make sure that you see the water overflowing down the side of the bath. Because water is transparent, it is not always easy to see and that is another reason why I have added an image of steam to the mnemonic.

In this particular sentence I have used an image of a golf range as opposed to a firing range, which I have used in previous sentences. Again, because I have used an image of a golf course with a lake, it is easy to image that there could well be a golf range in close proximity.

The image of the White House, as previously discussed, represents the word "constitutional" and the model railway represents the word "differences".

The image of jelly being eaten by a nun represents that there are approximately 22 words to be recalled.

Exercise 44

Recall the images that have been created and translate them back into the text. As you see the text state the words out loud. Repeat the exercise several times until you can state the text fluently and with ease.

Exercise 45

Recite all the text you have memorised thus far.

11th Sentence:

"Plato on the other hand had only three kinds of human beings."

The mnemonic scene:

I picture a kiwi fruit on a plate of potatoes, which is held by an ancient Greek philosopher in his right hand. With his other hand he pushes a Negro, a Chinaman and a Jew who are covered in beans.

Finally I see a tin squashing a kiwi fruit.

Explanation:

The kiwi fruit represents the 11th sentence. The plate of potatoes gives me the name "Plato". It is quite easy to picture an ancient Greek philosopher possibly wearing a white robe and a laurel leaf headdress. This imagery reinforces the mnemonic for the name Plato.

When creating mnemonic images with somebody using their hand it is often worthwhile using their other hand for the next mnemonic image. Most human beings have two hands and there is a natural curiosity that should lead us as to what might be happening in each hand. This will give us a natural progressing reference point. Again, please note that I look at the image of the Greek philosopher from left to right. I look at his right hand first and then his left. As discussed previously, in Western culture we read from left to right and this again gives us a natural progression

The image of a tin squashing a kiwi fruit tells me that there are approximately 12 words to recall in the 11th sentence.

Exercise 46

Recall the images that have been created and translate them back into the text. As you see the text state the words out loud. Repeat the exercise several times until you can state the text fluently and with ease.

Exercise 47

Recite all the text you have memorised thus far.

12th Sentence:

"How many kinds do you want?"

The mnemonic scene:

I see a lemon in the headdress of a Red Indian chief who is waving half a Swastika flag. With the flag he strikes Adam Faith who is mending his sock.

Finally I see a large shoe stamping on a lemon.

Explanation:

The lemon indicates that I am recalling the 12th sentence. The Red Indian chief's headdress gives me the word "how". The half swastika flag gives me the word "many" as previously discussed. The image of someone mending a sock gives me the word darner and the name Dana who sang a song called *All Kinds Of Everything* (as previously discussed) gives me the word "kinds". The image of the blond-haired Adam Faith gives me the words "do you want" (again, as previously discussed).

The shoe and lemon informs me that there are approximately 6 words in the 12th sentence.

Exercise 48

Recall the images that have been created and translate them back into the text. As you see the text state the words out loud. Repeat the exercise several times until you can state the text fluently and with ease.

Exercise 49

Recite all the text you have memorised thus far.

13th Sentence:

"Can there be a society without deviants?"

The mnemonic scene:

I picture a melon that rolls into a can, which spills its contents over a map and drowns a bee. The map is held by a group of naked old spinsters who are stitching the map to some DVDs, which are crawling in ants.

Finally I see a cow stamping on a melon.

Explanation:

The melon represents the 13th sentence. The can represents the word "can". The map represents the word "there" (as discussed) and the bee represents the word "be". The image of the naked old spinsters stitching gives me the words "society without". A group of people all partaking in the same activity, in this instance stitching or sewing, could be classed as a society. Seeing this particular group sewing gives me the first syllable (sew) in the word "society".

It is quite difficult to create a mnemonic image for an abstract word such as without. In such instances I usually create more than one image to reinforce the mnemonic. In this case I have used nakedness and spinsters, who are women without husbands. I have pictured old naked spinsters to make the scene a little more alarming.

Because I see these ladies as spinsters it necessarily follows that they are "without" husbands. The fact that they are naked indicates that they are "without" something.

DVDs are becoming increasingly more popular items. By seeing ants crawling on a DVD will give me the word "deviants". However, a DVD by itself appears as a silver disc and could prove to be ambiguous. Therefore, I suggest that you think of a DVD that you are familiar with and picture its packaging. Remember, such packaging is designed to stick in our minds and consequently can be used to our distinct advantage.

Notice how I get the spinsters to stitch the DVDs to the map. By making mnemonic images interact with each other as a chain of events simply makes them easier to recall.

If you experience difficulty in recalling a mnemonic image and your mind draws a blank, it is usually because you have failed to make your mnemonic images link, work or interact with each other sufficiently.

The image of a cow stamping on a melon informs me that there are approximately 7 words in the 13th sentence.

Exercise 50

Recall the images that have been created and translate them back into the text. As you see the text state the words out loud. Repeat the exercise several times until you can state the text fluently and with ease.

Exercise 51

Recite all the text you have memorised thus far.

14th Sentence

"Does the concept of self-actualisation make this question obsolete?"

The mnemonic scene:

I picture a prisoner with nuts on the arrows of his suit. He tries to brush them off with a yellow duster whilst holding a sceptre. In the other hand he is brandishing an axe with which he smashes a mirror. He also gazes at the reflection of his eyes in the mirror. Behind the mirror there is a roll of fabric that is being cut into the shape of a question mark by an athlete who is playing an oboe.

Finally, I see some peanuts.

Explanation:

The image of nuts informs me that it is the 14th sentence. The image of the prisoner gives me the first syllable of the word "concept". A common abbreviation for a convict is "con". The image for a prisoner or convict that I use is that of the iconic image of a suit covered with arrows. Notice how there is a physical action between the arrows and the nuts (i.e. dusting and brushing).

The sceptre represents the second syllable "cept", I have now created a mnemonic image for the word "concept".

An image of a duster represents the words "does the" as with a little imagination they sound similar. The word "does" is another abstract word and an image of a duster makes a suitable mnemonic to represent this word. If I want to recall the word "doesn't" or the words "does not", I picture a box of eggs, which usually contains a "dozen" eggs.

Another abstract word is "self". In this instance the word "self" is represented by a mirror because we can easily think of looking out ourselves in a mirror. The image of an axe will give me the word "actualisation". Seeing an image of a mirror and an axe should suffice to give me the words "self-actualisation". It is not necessary to create a mnemonic image for each syllable. However, in the mnemonic scene I did mention seeing the eyes of the convict in the reflection of the mirror. This was just to help reinforce the word "actualisation"(actual-eyes-ation).

Another abstract word is "make", so I have pictured a roll of fabric to represent this word. The image of the fabric makes me think of the word "fabricate" which means to make.

It is quite easy to imagine a piece of fabric being cut into a shape or pattern. In this case the fabric is cut into the shape of a question mark to represent the word "question". Whenever you see some action being taken, such as cutting, it is worthwhile asking who or what is causing the action. In this instance there is an athlete playing an oboe, which gives me the word "obsolete".

Again, in the above mnemonic scene the syllabic mnemonic images may not necessarily appear in the correct sequence. However, as previously discussed, our subconscious mind will make sense of the order with a little practice.

The image of peanuts informs me that there are approximately 9 words in the 14th sentence. Notice how I have combined two images (i.e. peas and nuts) to form one image of peanuts. This idea of combining two images to make just one image makes a very powerful mnemonic. It is always worthwhile spending a little time to see if you can make such combinations. You will be quite surprised at how frequently such opportunities will present themselves.

Exercise 52

Recall the images that have been created and translate them back into the text. As you see the text state the words out loud. Repeat the exercise several times until you can state the text fluently and with ease.

Exercise 53

Recite all the text you have memorised thus far.

15th Sentence:

"If you accept the widest range of individual differences and the pluralism of characters and talents, then there is a society that in effect accepts much (or all) of human nature."

The mnemonic scene:

I picture the TV detective Kojak licking an orange lollipop whilst riding a unicycle and brandishing an axe and sceptre. Whilst trying to balance he absent-mindedly rides into a river estuary. On the other side of the river there is a firing range with two Hindis standing back to back, each holding a pistol, with a model railway passing between them. Along the track of the railway is a plough being pushed by two old farmers followed by some actors in costume. Suddenly one of the actors is lifted into the air by the talons of a large bird of prey.

The bird of prey is also holding an egg timer in its beak, which it drops onto a map that is held by a group of people sewing and drinking tea. The group is watching Mrs Thatcher cover an axe and sceptre with disinfectant from a bottle. She picks up the sceptre and smashes it into a window of a pet shop and the glass shatters all over the animals. One of the animals is holding an oar, on which is balanced a human skull, which is covered with flowers, weeds, birds and bees.

I finally picture an orange mat.

Explanation:

The image of Kojak gives me the word "if" because the actor who played Kojak, Telly Savalas, had a hit single in the 1970s called *If*. Kojak was famous for carrying a lollipop, in this instance I coloured the lollipop orange to represent the 15th sentence. In fact I actually pictured an orange on the end of a stick so that it looked like a lollipop.

Incidentally, the opening lyric of the song *If* is: "If a picture paints a thousand words". This is so true in the world of mnemonics.

The unicycle gives me the word "you" and the axe and sceptre gives me the word "accept". The river estuary gives me the word "widest". This is because the mouth of a river is usually at its widest at the estuary. Also the word "estuary" contains the letters "est", which is the suffix of widest.

Whenever you use a river for your mnemonic scene it is worthwhile looking on the bank for a reference point for the next mnemonic image.

The mnemonics for the words "range", "individual", "differences", "pluralism" and "character" have been discussed previously.

Sensational Memory

The talons of the bird of prey suit my purpose as it sounds like the word "talents". Whenever I see such a bird picking up something with its feet, I then look to see what it might be holding in its beak. In this instance the bird of prey is holding an egg timer. The egg timer represents the word "then". Again, the word "then" is very abstract but yet a commonly used word in text. The word "then" pertains to time and very tenuously sounds like the word "hen". Since hens lay eggs I combine the concept of an egg and time to create a mnemonic image of an egg timer.

We have already discussed the mnemonic image of a map to represent the word "there". The group of people sewing and drinking tea represents the word "society". We have also discussed the mnemonic image of Mrs Thatcher as representing the word "that".

The bottle of disinfectant is a little obscure but in this case it represents the words "in effect". Occasionally we have to grant ourselves a little licence. The axe and sceptre again represent the word "accept".

The word "much" is another abstract word but it will frequently appear in text. I have chosen to use an image of a pet shop, which reminds me of the song *How Much Is That Doggie In The Window*, to represent the word "much". This will prove to be a useful mnemonic as we can place various objects, articles and create drama in or around a pet shop.

The various animals covered in glass in this instance represent the word "all". The image of the oar, as previously discussed, represents the word "or". Again our subconscious mind will naturally work out the correct sequence of the words to be recalled. The image of the human skull covered in bees, birds and flowers represents the words "human nature".

I simply picture an orange mat to inform me that there are approximately 31 words to recall.

Notice how, in this instance, I do not actually picture an orange, but simply colour the mat orange. This simply compacts the information required.

Exercise 54

Recall the images that have been created and translate them back into the text. As you see the text state the words out loud. Repeat the exercise several times until you can state the text fluently and with ease.

Exercise 55

Recite all the text you have memorised thus far.

16th Sentence:

"Does self-actualisation mean in effect the acceptance of idiosyncrasy or of deviants?"

The mnemonic scene:

I picture someone holding a pear in a duster whilst polishing an axe and looking at their reflection in the shiny blade. The axe is being held by the Dickensian character Scrooge. In his other hand he is shaking a bottle of disinfectant over an axe and sceptre because they are covered with ants.

A village idiot picks up the axe and places it in a sink. He picks his nose whilst holding a DVD in his mouth, which is also covered in ants.

Finally, I see a tin of pears.

Explanation:

The pear informs me that it is the 16th sentence. The duster gives me the word "does". The reflection in the blade of the axe gives me the words "self-actualisation". When you see this particular mnemonic image you will see its many features in just one image. With practice you will be able to quite simply work out the correct sequence of the words in an instant,.

The Dickensian character Scrooge gives me the word "mean". This is because Scrooge was renowned for being a "mean" miser. I picture him wearing gloves that have his bare fingers protruding from the fingers of the glove.

The bottle of disinfectant again gives me the word "in effect". The axe and sceptre crawling with ants gives me the word "acceptance".

We have previously discussed the image of a village idiot (you may recall that I pictured a court jester in the 4th sentence) and a sink to give me the word "idiosyncrasy".

The image of the village idiot picking his nose makes me think of orifice, which gives me the words "or of". The use of the village idiot's mouth also reinforces the idea of the word "orifice".

This mnemonic may seem to be contrived but the point is that it works for me. I have no doubt that with practice you will spot similar opportunities that will work to great effect for you in future. Ironically, it is these contrived mnemonics that work best because the mental thinking process makes them memorable.

The DVD crawling with ants, as previously discussed, gives me the word "deviants".

The tin of pears informs me that there are approximately 12 words in the 16th sentence.

Exercise 56

Recall the images that have been created and translate them back into the text. As you see the text state the words out loud. Repeat the exercise several times until you can state the text fluently and with ease.

Exercise 57

Recite all the text you have memorised thus far.

17th Sentence:

"To what extent?"

The mnemonic scene:

I picture a cucumber with two light bulbs flashing attached to an extension lead.

Finally, I see my mother slicing a cucumber.

Explanation:

The cucumber informs that I'm focussing on the 17th sentence. The two light bulbs give me the words "To what". The word "what" is another abstract word that is frequently used in text. However, a light bulb's power is measured in Watts and this fact will give me a useful mnemonic that is worth adding to the Mnemonic Vocabulary.

The extension lead gives me the word "extent". It is easy to make an association with an electric light bulb and an electric extension cable. This is an added bonus that reinforces the mnemonic. However, you may have noticed how mnemonics develop a theme and pattern within themselves.

The image of my mother slicing a cucumber informs me that there only three words in the 17th sentence.

Exercise 58

Recall the images that have been created and translate them back into the text. As you see the text state the words out loud. Repeat the exercise several times until you can state the text fluently and with ease.

Exercise 59

Recite all the entire passage of text.

Below is a list of the mnemonic images that may be useful for memorising future text. They are not set in stone and you may, of course, prefer to create your own images. In fact, the ones you create for yourself will be easier to recall. Your own thinking process and creativity will make your power of recall work more efficiently.

Mnemonic Vocabulary

Actual - Hacksaw cutting into a jewel

Allow - Megaphone (aloud - allowed or allow)

Among - Monk

ble (suffix) - Bull

But - Butter

Choice - Choc-ice.

Does the - Duster

e.g. - Broken Egg

etc.- Yul Brynner

Individual - Turban

Knowledge - Owl (the word "knowledge" contains the letters o w l).

Many - Half a Swastika (Ger many)

No - Ursula Andress / snorkel and mask

Now - Stopwatch

Our - Hourglass

People - Kaleidoscope (peephole)

Seem - Coal (seam)

Senile - Twisted Sea Lion

Some - Calculator

There - Map

Variation - Fairy riding a Dalmatian

Very - Fairy

What - Light bulb (watts)

Wide - Window

Whole - Golf hole (with flag).

You - Unicycle

Chapter 17

It is a common problem that when someone is introduced to a stranger they instantly forget the name of the person they have just met. This may cause embarrassment or a distraction from memorising other important information that the stranger may have.

How do we overcome this problem? Firstly, it is not really a problem to ask the person to state their name again. The chances are the stranger has been in a similar situation and will sympathise with you. In fact, they may be pleased that you took the trouble to learn their name correctly.

The reason why I make this point is to try to eliminate any fear you may have of memorising someone's name. In such instances, confidence is an important key to success. Remember that when you meet someone, they will probably be anxious to try to remember your name too. There is a strong likelihood that they will not know the mnemonic techniques that you are about to learn.

With careful study and a little practice you will soon be able to justify your newfound confidence. It will not be long before people are complimenting you on your powers of recall.

The first step to take on hearing someone's name during an introduction is to repeat his or her name out loud. For example, someone may introduce themself by saying, 'Hello my name is John'.

You simply reply, 'I'm pleased to meet you, John.'

This simple action takes at least two thinking processes to achieve. Your aural faculties have to take in the information and then vocal faculties are made to act on that information. The mental energy involved makes the person's name more memorable.

This technique may be suitable for recalling one or two names during a brief introduction. However, it may not be suitable for when we are introduced to several people.

What makes the ability of recalling names difficult for most people is that names are usually intangible and often do not have any meaning. Although some names may have an original meaning, for most people the meaning has been lost in the sands of time.

With a little strategic imagination we can easily overcome this problem. We need to create a mnemonic image to the sound of a person's name. This is not a problem if someone is called Robin or Rose, but rarely are we afforded such luxury.

So let's take another look at the introduction of John. You may recall that when we were learning the Mnemonic Alphabet we created a mnemonic for King John.

The mnemonic image we created was that of a toilet seat because an American slang term for a toilet is "John". As you hear the name John and begin to repeat his name vocally, picture him with a toilet seat around his neck. To reinforce the mnemonic, cover the imaginary toilet seat with the same material as he is wearing (e.g. a tweed jacket).

There is a problem with making mnemonics with people's clothing, spectacles and hairstyles, as people change them from time to time. However, usually making a strong initial mnemonic is sufficient for our natural memory to utilise its powers of facial recognition.

We will later look at ways to memorise names and faces by creating mnemonics with more permanent features. In the meantime, let's look at a few popular names and create a visual mnemonic for them before looking at ways to attach them to people.

Here are few popular names listed in alphabetical order. Some of the mnemonic images may be obvious and some a little more obscure. However, studying the list will get your creative juices flowing and give you some suitable ideas:

Aaron - Sweater

Andy - Glove (handy)

Angela - Angel

Barbara - Barbed wire

Bob - Goldfish (this is because a goldfish appears to be calling the name Bob in a fish tank)

Bill - Banknote

Chris - Cross

Charles - King Charles Spaniel (long floppy ears).

Claire - Chocolate éclair.

Dave - Surfboard (Dave rhymes with wave)

David - DVD

Deborah - Zebra

Elaine - Country lane

Elizabeth - Busy Lizzy (flowering plant)

Edward - Piece of wood.

Frank - Tank

Fred - Frog or red.

Fiona - A ticket or fee. This is similar to Bill but you can mentally select two different types of ticket to represent each name.

Graham - Greyhound

Gerry - A German helmet or a Jerrycan

Grace - Grass

Henry - Hen

Harry - Hairy

Hilary - Hill

Irene - Ice rink

Isaac - Ice in a sack

Imogene - Mirror (mirror image).

Jack - Union Jack flag

Julie - Jewellery

Jennifer - Jellyfish

Kim - Kimono (Japanese garment)

Ken - Dog kennel

Keith - Key

Linda - Glove (lend a hand)

Lucy - Elastic (loose elastic)

Larry - Hat (song *Hats off to Larry*)

Malcolm - Milk

Michael - Mackerel

Mandy - Mango

Mohammed - Lawnmower

Nigel - Hair gel

Nora - Mouse (gnaw)

Nathan - Donkey (neigh is a sound made by a donkey)

Oliver - Olive

Oscar - Oscar Trophy

Omar - Mars Bar

Peter - Pizza

Philip - Screwdriver

Paul - Ball

Quentin - Cucumber (there are so few names beginning with the letter Q that an image of a cucumber is sufficient to prompt the name Quentin)

Raquel - Racquet

Richard - Coins (Rich)

Roger - Skull and Crossbones (Jolly Roger)

Stephen - Steel fence

Stanley - Stanley knife or a Stan Laurel Derby hat

Susan - Saucepan

Thomas - Tomato

Tom - Sliced Tomato (the slice indicates that Tom's name is probably Thomas but prefers to be called Tom).

Tina - Concertina (musical instrument)

Ursula - Hearse

Vernon - Fern leaf

Vera - Compass (Veering North)

Vivienne - Spanish Flag (*Viva España*)

Walter - Water

Wayne - Wine

Wendy - House (Wendy House)

Yvonne - Scales (even)

Zara - Russian hat (Tsar)

Similar methods can be used for creating mnemonics for surnames. There are several websites on the Internet that give origins for both first names and surnames. It would not be a waste of time to study some of the most common names where an immediate mnemonic image does not spring to mind. However, Internet access will probably not be available when we first meet someone, and we will need to quickly create a suitable mnemonic without any external resource.

Let's look in detail at how we can apply mnemonics for remembering names and faces by looking at the following photographs. I hasten to add that the names are completely fictitious. However, I have not shied away from using difficult names to ensure that the task ahead is challenging.

Initially, it may appear time-consuming to sit and study the whys and wherefores of how the following mnemonics are created. However, despite the complexities of what you are

Sensational Memory

about to learn, with a little practice you will be able to create such mnemonics in a matter of seconds during a brief introduction. Furthermore, you may be surprised at how effective your powers of recall are when put to the test.

There are 52 names and faces below for which I have created mnemonics. Although creating mnemonics is a very personal creative process please try to follow and understand the whys and wherefores as to how I have created these mnemonics. The reasoning behind them will help you when you come to creating your own mnemonics when meeting new people for the first time.

Once you have studied a group of ten names and faces try to recall them from pictures placed in random order.

Faces 1 to 10

Aaron Smith.

The first thing you may notice about Aaron Smith is that his forehead slopes forward from top to bottom. This part of his face appears paler than the rest of his face. Let's use this fact to our advantage. We can use a mnemonic image of Aran wool (which is traditionally white in colour) to represent the name Aaron.

Here we can make a quick musical mnemonic by hearing the tune *Whiter Shade of Pale*. Although it is not totally necessary it would be an advantage to be able to hear this tune in your mind as you study this person's face.

Imagine that there is a rolled-up Aran sweater resting on the person's head. Suddenly part of the sweater unfurls and covers his forehead and eyes, causing his eyes to blink. This action will draw attention to his eyes.

Each of his eyes are shaped almost like the horn of an anvil. An anvil is a tool of a blacksmith and it is this image that will give us the surname Smith. In this instance, the blackness of the eyes can trigger the word blacksmith.

There are a couple of other general mnemonics we can use to help us. The mnemonics we have used already can be termed as Black and White. We can also think of the expression, "Pulling the wool over his eyes".

Some of these mnemonics may seem tenuous or farfetched. However, our minds do naturally make such associations. What we do as mnemonists is find them and pay particular attention to them and put them to use.

Floyd Rogers

Sometimes it may be easier to put the cart before the horse. In this instance, we will look at creating a mnemonic for the surname first. It is not an uncommon fact that a pirate skull and crossbones flag was also known as a Jolly Roger. So a Jolly Roger flag will serve as a mnemonic image for the name Rogers.

The Jolly Roger flag traditionally has a black background with white skull and crossbones. However, since this person is probably of Afro-Caribbean origin we reverse the colours so the flag has a white background and black skull and crossbones. This reversal of colours is a very powerful technique.

The name Floyd sounds similar to the word "flied". The word "flied" can be the past tense of the word "fly". In this case, we can make an association with a flag and flying. However, because this association is not immediate with the name Floyd it is advisable to make another visual mnemonic to cue the sound of the name. In this instance, try to picture flies buzzing around the flag.

People of Afro-Caribbean origin are not always easily distinguishable from each other at first glance. Therefore, it is important to pay particular attention to the size and shape of such people's face and head.

With a little imagination we can imagine this person's head as being shaped like an Easter egg. With the word egg we can think of fried egg which sounds like Floyd egg. With a little practice, play on words comes with ease and will prove to be very effective.

Andy James

The first thing I notice about this person is the tightness of his skin. It's almost as if his skin is being pulled back or a strong wind is pushing it back. When you see a prominent feature try to give a reason as to what might have caused that feature to come about. The reason you give yourself may be completely fictional, ridiculous or bizarre but nevertheless look for a cause and effect.

We can use a mnemonic image of a rubber glove for the name Andy (Handy). Imagine that a rubber glove has been stretched over this person's face and is causing him a breathing difficulty. The breathing difficulty will draw attention to the person's mouth.

Notice how there is quite a large distance between his top and bottom lip and yet there is no gap between his bottom and top teeth. This inherently means that the lips have a large circumference, which we shall use to our advantage shortly.

We can think of a mnemonic image of jam to give us the name James. This is simply because jam consists of the first three letters of the name James. Let's imagine spreading red jam around the lips to exaggerate them and to give us the surname James.

Although I do not wish to encourage you to make mnemonics with features that are changeable (hairstyle, clothing etc.) there is no harm in using them so long as you do not become dependent on them.

In this instance we can imagine the tufts of hair sticking up at the top of the head as the fingers of the rubber glove. We could imagine that his spectacles are made from the bottoms of jam jars.

Angela Cook

This person has very long and straight cheekbones. Imagine placing an angel's wing on each side of her face. The angel's wings will give us the name Angela. Notice also that her eyes seem to have a natural tendency to glance downwards. Her eyebrows are not straight and could be described as arched. This will also give us an association with the word archangel.

For the surname Cook we can think of a tall chef's hat. The girl's head is almost the same shape as a chef's hat. Imagine a large chef's hat being placed over her head so that it completely covers her face and rests on her shoulders.

As you picture the chef's hat over her head, imagine those angel wings trying to flap under the hat. See the sides of the hat pulsate in and out as the wings try to open.

Barbara Jones

We can use a mnemonic image of barbed wire to give us the name Barbara. This person has piercing blue eyes. Her blue eyes appear to be even more piercing due to the very fair complexion of her skin Let's imagine that her blue eyes are pierced on the spikes of barbed wire.

She has quite a long straight nose although quite bulbous at the lower part. This shape is very similar to a dog's bone. Bones rhymes with Jones, which makes a suitable mnemonic for the surname.

Bill Clark

The distance between this person's top and bottom eyelid is very narrow. It makes his eyes appear almost as one horizontal line across his face. Let's allow ourselves a little licence and take advantage of this feature.

A banknote makes a suitable mnemonic for the name Bill. Although the term is chiefly American, most English speaking people have heard of a dollar bill and have a vague image of what one looks like.

The origin of the name Clark is that of someone who is a clerk (English people pronounce it as clark) or cleric. Given this fact we can easily accept that a regular tool for a clerk could be a pen.

Imagine a dollar bill rolled around a pen. Then imagine the pen and bill being pushed through his nose, just above the bridge. This imaginary image should substitute the eyes.

However, a spark will make a suitable rhyming mnemonic. I know of more than one person with the surname Clark who have been given the nickname Sparky. To use this mnemonic simply imagine sparks that match the colour of the person's eyes flying out from the ends of the rolled-up bill.

Claire Harris

A mnemonic image of a chocolate éclair will give us the name Claire. The question is how do we make an attachment between a chocolate éclair and this person's face?

If we draw an imaginary line around the eyebrows and around the top of the cheekbones, we can begin to see a similar shape to that of an oblong chocolate éclair. Place an imaginary chocolate éclair into that space, almost like placing a piece into a jigsaw puzzle.

To animate the images just imagine that every time the girl blinks, she squeezes more and more cream out of the éclair. You could also imagine her eyes in the cream like glacé cherries.

The surname does present a few problems. We could think of the Eiffel Tower to represent Paris, which rhymes with Harris. However, there are several people who's surname is actually Paris. This could cause confusion and lead to a mistake.

Out of courtesy to the reader, I have tried to avoid using crudity and vulgarity. However, when strategically placed, especially with humour, they make the most powerful of mnemonic tools.

There is a problem with using crudity and vulgarity in that, because they make such powerful mnemonics, there is a danger that the imagery may overshadow and distract from other important details you may need to recall.

The mnemonic image I have created for Harris is hairy arse. I think of one of those plastic bums that are sold in joke shops and imagine it being covered with hair.

As we have already thought about someone's facial cheeks we can easily make an association with the word cheeks and think of a person's bottom. This wordplay will give us a link between the person's first name and surname.

Place the hairy arse over the person's mouth and imagine the cream from the éclair running into it.

Dave Evans

We can think of a diver's mask for the name Dave. This is simply because the word "dive" appears very similar to the name Dave. Diver's masks are usually shaped to appear wider across the face than longer. We will make use of this fact in a moment.

In this instance, the person's face appears quite long as he has long cheekbones and a high forehead. Let's turn our imaginary diving mask 90 degrees so that it covers the whole of the person's face. Picture the mask nestling around the top of his hairline all the way round to the bottom of his chin.

This idea of rotating things to fit something else is a very useful technique. Our minds like to play with shapes. We learnt from a very early age that square pegs don't fit round holes. Odd and unusual things stick out in our minds. Just simply by using mental energy and toying with ideas makes things memorable.

For the surname Evans we could think of stars and moons, which we can associate with the heavens. Evans and heavens sound very similar and this image will make a suitable mnemonic.

Wherever possible we should try to make the mnemonic images interact so that we can link the first name with the surname. We can easily associate air bubbles coming from a diver underwater and floating upwards. In this instance, let's substitute air bubbles with stars and moons and see them floating upwards from the person's mouth.

Edward Carrington

A piece of wood makes a suitable mnemonic image for the name Edward, as there are not many other names with that sound. We need to look at this person's face and decide where we could fit a small block of wood. I would suggest placing it over the eyes. This is because a vague oblong shape is outlined between the bottom of his eyebrows and just inside the lens of his spectacles. Transfer the lines on the side of his face on to the block of wood and think of them as grains in the wood.

Another way to remind us that the person's name is Edward is by looking at the overall general shape of his head and think of it as an acorn.

The surname Carrington can be easily broken into three syllables that make the three words Car Ring Ton. To strengthen the mnemonic we can imagine a toy wooden car to remind us of the name Edward (wood). We can place the wooden car on the block of wood and imagine a ring attached to the back of the car as a tow bar. Then imagine the ring attached to a ton weight.

Feel the car straining against the weight and see the wooden wheels skidding on the surface of the block of wood.

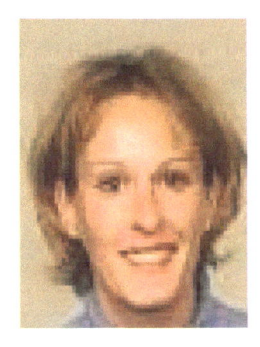

Elaine Gorman

Possibly the most striking feature of this person is her brown eyes set in the fair complexion of her face.

The name Elaine can be represented by a mnemonic image of a country lane. Imagine one of those country roads that has grass growing down the middle. Imagine this person's face set in the grass every few yards. Her eyes could be cat's eyes in the middle of the road.

The surname Gorman will need an expansive imagination to create a workable mnemonic.

In such instances it is worth doing some wordplay and look at the person's face to see if we can make a story. Notice how this person's face is quite narrow from cheek to cheek. Let's see how we can make use of this fact to make a mnemonic for the surname Gorman.

The name Gorman rhymes with doorman. I picture a bouncer from a nightclub kneeling on the grass of the country lane and squashing this person's face by pushing her cheeks towards the centre of her face. This image can be repeated every few yards along the country lane.

To remind us that the surname is Gorman and not Doorman I think of the doorman squashing that person's face and using G-force.

Sensational Memory

Random faces 1 to 10. Recall the correct name for each face

Chris Hare

Faces 11 to- 20

Elizabeth Davis

The name Elizabeth is synonymous with two Queens of England. In this instance we can think of an image of a queen's crown to represent the name Elizabeth. We could simply picture a crown upon this person's head but imagining things placed in an unorthodox manner will make a stronger mnemonic.

Instead of placing the crown on top of the head, imagine it being placed around the perimeter of the person's face. Imagine the bottom rim of the crown being malleable and fitted to the shape of the face.

The Davis Cup is a famous tennis competition and it's not necessary to be a follower of tennis to know of its title. Simply picture any type of cup to represent the name Davis or Davies. It does not have to be an image of the actual tennis trophy. An image of a teacup would suit our purpose.

The surname Davis or Davies is quite common and you may meet more than one person at any given time who share that surname. Should such an occasion arise then you can picture different types of cups to identify each person.

Although a large silver trophy would make an excellent mnemonic, in this instance, let's use an image of a pair of teacups. Imagine the mouths of two teacups placed over the person's eyes. Imagine the rim of the cups touching just below the eyebrows and above the cheekbones, around the eyes.

To link the first name with the surname we could imagine another cup hanging from its handle on one of the prongs of the crown. Picture it swinging to and fro as movement makes things more memorable.

Bharat Patel

The name Bharat rhymes with parrot, which is a bird that we can easily picture in our minds. However, we need to think how we can attach an image of a parrot to this person's face to make an effective mnemonic.

If we look at the face in general it is round in shape. However, the eyebrows are not arched but quite straight. With a little imagination we could imagine a parrot perched on the eyebrows. If we picture a blue parrot this will help remind us that the person's name begins with the letter B as the colour blue begins with the same letter. We could also picture a bee buzzing around the parrot for the same purpose.

The surname Patel is similar to the word petal. If we look at the person's face, the rounded cheeks are quite prominent. This would be a suitable point to place a petal.

To link the first name with the surname we can imagine the parrot leaning forward from its perch (eyebrows) and picking up the petal with its beak from the person's cheek.

Curtis Wallace

The name Curtis sounds similar to curtains. Although this person's face is quite rounded in shape the cheekbones and sides of the face are relatively long and straight. Let's imagine that the sides of the face are the edge of a pair of curtains closing in on the face.

The surname Wallace sounds similar to wallet. Imagine a wallet bulging with banknotes is attached to either side of the imaginary curtains. Imagine the wallet opening and closing as the curtains open and close. Most of us have to be mindful of money and seeing images of cash makes us pay attention. For this reason an image of money makes a powerful mnemonic.

Frank Ferguson

One of the prominent features of this person's face is the long straight nose. We could substitute this nose with a frankfurter sausage to give us the name Frank.

The other prominent feature of this face is the dark area around the eyes. The surname Ferguson sounds similar to fungus. Fungus is associated with mushrooms. The undersides of mushroom tops are also dark. Picture the underside of mushrooms and place them over the person's eyes.

Deborah Elliot

The popular name Deborah can be easily represented by the distinctive black and white stripes of a zebra, which rhymes with the name. This person's forehead is quite prominent as it appears to be a flat oblong shape. If we imagine the zebra stripes filling that space we will have an effective mnemonic for the person's first name.

We can keep an animal theme for the surname Elliot by thinking of an elephant. The bulbous nose on this face also appears quite prominent. If we can imagine an elephant's trunk attached to the nose we will also have a powerful mnemonic for the person's surname.

Fiona Hamilton

The popular first name Fiona does not lend itself easily to create a quick mnemonic. However, simply by using a thinking process and making an extra effort this will make the face more memorable as and when it is required to recall the person's name.

This person's face appears to be very round in shape and this may be because her hair appears to be tied back. However, her face may appear differently if her hair was let down. For this reason we need to look for features which are unlikely to change with the passing of time.

It is possible to draw a circular outline from the chin and around the eyebrows. The eyebrows are rounded as opposed to straight which helps create an overall circular shape to the face.

Let's make use of this circular shape and imagine it to be a large coin or token that might be used to put into a slot machine to pay a fee. The word "fee" will give us a mnemonic for the first syllable of the name Fiona. It is not necessary to create a mnemonic for the other syllables, as there is not likely to be another girl's first name beginning with the syllable sound of fee. In fact, it would be fair to say that many ladies with the name Fiona simply have their name abbreviated to Fi.

The eyes of this person's face are dark and deeply set. By substituting these dark eyes with two slices of ham, we will have something to trigger the first syllable of the surname Hamilton. This again would probably be sufficient for our purpose.

If necessary, we could take it a stage further to get a mnemonic for the second syllable. Making use of opposites is a powerful memory technique. Seeing something pleasant that suddenly does something undisputedly unpleasant sends a jolt through our metabolism and creates a lasting impression.

The person's mouth appears to be an attractive feature of her face. However, if we were to picture her suddenly vomiting (ill) this would be a strong mnemonic. Unpleasant and distasteful images make powerful mnemonics but should be used carefully as they may overshadow other important information.

Nadia Chopra

The first name Nadia may not easily trigger off a similar sound of an everyday word. However, the word Nadir is a term meaning the lowest point of the universe and will prove to be useful. This person's eyes are a very prominent feature of her face. In this instance we can think of those eyes as two black holes in space that will draw us down into the Nadir of the universe.

Often a word will spark off a theme that can be linked to the face or the name. In this case, the word Nadir has connotations of space and so do black holes. A theme can give us a foundation on which to lay our mnemonic storylines.

The surname Chopra can be represented by an image of an axe (chopper). This person's nose is long and narrow. We can imagine it being the front edge of the blade of an axe. Let's make a short storyline by imagining that the axe has split a black hole into two.

Isaac Lewin

The most prominent feature of this person's face is the black oblong shape around the eyes. If we think of this area as a block of black ice we can make an association with an ice axe. An ice axe will give us a mnemonic image for the fist name Isaac. To animate the mnemonic, imagine that ice axe smashing into the block of ice and causing a fissure across the area around the eyes.

To help create a mnemonic for the surname Lewin we can dabble with a little informality. British readers will be familiar with the informal name for a toilet "loo" and toilet tissues being referred to as "loo paper". Fortunately, once idiosyncratic cultural differences are pointed out to us, they seem to stay in our memory, particularly if the idiosyncrasy has a slightly comical overtone.

Given that we will use a roll of loo paper as a mnemonic image to represent the surname Lewin, let's look at how we might attach the image to the person's face.

There are two distinctive lines that run down at an angle from either side of the nose. We can imagine these lines to be pieces of string, which pass through the loo roll to hold it in place. Imagine the loo roll covering the mouth and chin area. Furthermore, imagine the lips being the first leaf of tissue that is pulled and torn off at an appropriate time.

It may be necessary to create a mnemonic for the second syllable of the surname. If we look at the person's chin we will see that it has a dimple. Let's imagine an inn sign slotted into that groove and that it swings to and fro. To reinforce the mnemonic we can think of a sound in rhyming with chin. This in itself may not be strong enough but the thought of a chin may draw our attention to the dimple and trigger off an image of an inn sign.

Simon Lewis

On hearing the name Simon one could be forgiven for thinking of the children's nursery rhyme *Simple Simon*. If we think of Simple Simon we may involuntarily continue the line, "met a pieman going to the fair." In which case an image of a pie will make a suitable mnemonic to represent the first name Simon.

The pink complexion of the person's face is not that different from the pink colour of the inside of a pork pie. This alone should suffice to put the name Simon to this face.

The surname Lewis is not that different from the surname Lewin, which we have already discussed. We can place a loo roll over the forehead to give us the first syllable. The second syllable can be given by looking at the eyebrows. Think of the eyebrows as being one continuous line that forms a snake. The sound that a snake makes is called a hiss and it is this sound that will give us the second syllable. Imagine the snake (eyebrows) slithering through the tube in the loo roll.

Zara Littlewood

For the first name Zara we can think of a Russian tsar. The eyes and forehead are quite prominent features and if we imagine a Russian fur hat covering these two features, we will have a suitable mnemonic image to serve our purpose.

We could substitute the nose with a miniature bonsai tree to represent the surname Littlewood.

Because the nose is not a particularly prominent feature we can imagine the leaves of the bonsai tree brushing against the fur of the Russian hat. This will help recall both names once we recall any part of the mnemonic.

Chris Hare

Random faces 11 to 20. Recall the correct name for each face.

Faces 21 to 30.

Kirk Anderson

We are now going to deal with the sometimes difficult problem of identical twins. The trick is to exaggerate any one difference there may be and create a mnemonic around the difference.

For the sake of convenience, let's deal with the surname that they share first. The first two syllables of the surname sound similar to the word "Under". So if we visualise underpants or underwear this will give a mnemonic for the name Anderson.

However, we need to think of two distinctly different types of underpants and attached them or associate them with the facial differences. If we look at the two pairs of eyes we will see that Kirk's eyes are narrower than Brian's whose eyes are almost square.

As Kirk's eyes are narrower let's substitute his eyes with a pair briefs and as Brian's eyes are larger and more square let's substitute his eyes with a pair of boxer shorts.

To make a stronger mnemonic let's imagine Kirk's briefs are a khaki colour. This will remind us that his name starts with the letter K. For Brian let's make his boxer shorts blue to remind us his name starts with the letter B.

Brian Anderson

Let's deal more thoroughly with the first names of the Anderson twins. In this instance, we can see that their noses are different. Kirk's nose is narrower and the nostrils are hardly noticeable. Brian's nose is broader and the nostrils are flared and more exposed.

The first name Kirk has similar sounding consonants to the word "Cake". So let's substitute his nose with a slice of cake that is the same shape and size as the nose.

The first name Brian is anagram of the word "Brain". Let's imagine that we can look up those exposed nostrils and see his brain.

Just to add another mnemonic, we can think of Brian's nose as being more a like boxer's nose, which we can make an association with boxer shorts that are substituting his eyes.

Thomas Jerome

The first name Tom can be represented by a mnemonic image of a tomato. However, if we have an image of a pair of tomatoes, the idea of pluralism will give us an indication that the person's name ends with the letter S, as usually pluralized words in the English language end with the letter S. A pair of tomatoes will give us a suitable mnemonic for the first name Thomas.

If we look at the outline of this person's face we can see that the bottom half is broader than the top. For this reasons the cheeks appear to be quite some distance apart. If we were to place a tomato on each cheek this will create a suitable mnemonic for the first name.

The first syllable of the surname Jerome sounds similar to chair. In this instance, we need to stretch our imaginations and look for wider associations of a chair. Ignoring the fact that this face is bearded it still appears as if the chin and lower face are very broad.

Let's take the outline of the lower face and chin and think of it as a seat of a chair. Then take this idea of a chair a stage further and think of it as a Roman emperor's throne. The idea of a

Roman emperor will give us a strong association with Rome to give us the second syllable of the surname.

If we think of the tomatoes as being at the front of the armrests, as part of the ornamentation of the throne, we can link the first name and surname together.

Fred Smith

One noticeable feature of this person's face is the narrowness of the eyes. In this modern day and age most people are familiar with infrared. Infrared will give us a mnemonic for the first name Fred. Let's imagine two beams of red light being projected from those narrow eyes.

The surname has been dealt with by using an image of an anvil (blacksmith). Again we can substitute the person's nose with the horn of an anvil. However, to link the first name and surname picture the infrared light touching either side of the nose.

Mohammed Khan

For this person's face we are going to focus on the triangular shape formed by the lines either side of the nose. Let's imagine this triangle forms part of a lawnmower to give us the first syllable of the first name. Often just one mnemonic for the first syllable is enough to give us an indication as to the complete name. However, it is worthwhile taking a little time to create a mnemonic for the other syllables. This is especially true if we can make the mnemonic images for the syllables interact with each other. In this instance, we can think of the lawnmower being hammered to give us the remaining syllables. Simply picture and hear a hammer striking a lawnmower.

For the surname, we are going to use the same lines and draw an imaginary line continuing around the bottom of the broad chin. Let's imagine this shape forms a watering can. The word "can" sounds similar to Khan and this should be suitable for our purpose.

In addition, it appears that the left-hand side of the face is lower than the right. We can imagine this being the watering can being tipped to pour water. There is also a slight dimple in the left cheek and if we imagine water pouring from this dimple the imaginary action will make the mnemonic stronger.

Although we have used the same facial features for both first name and surname, this will not matter as the mnemonic images have a common theme. That is to say that both images are items that are likely to be found in a garden.

Nathan Urqhart

As mentioned previously, it is important to ignore features that may change (beards, spectacles etc.). For this face we are going to stretch our imaginations and look at wider associations.

For the name Nathan we can think of a donkey because "nay" is the sound that a donkey makes. This will, of course, give us the first syllable of the first name. But how do we make a link with this face and a donkey? If you have ridden a donkey or seen one from close quarters you may recall that donkeys have two dark stripes on their backs that form a cross.

If we think of the face as an aerial view of a donkey's back, we can draw a vertical straight line by extending an imaginary line from the person's straight nose.

Sensational Memory

We can draw a horizontal line from the eyebrows. As the eyebrows are slightly rounded we can imagine the lines continuing around the donkey's waist.

The narrowness of the nose makes the cheekbones seem more prominent. Given this fact, we can make use of this for the surname. Imagine those cheekbones to be two bald heads. They are bald because they have had their hair cut. Hair cut is a similar enough sound to give us the surname Urqhart.

To link the first name with the surname imagine seeing an aerial view of a donkey saddled with two decapitated bald heads.

Raquel Danson

The shape of this person's face is not dissimilar from the shape of the face of a tennis or badminton racquet. This, of course, gives us an easy mnemonic for the first name Raquel.

The surname Danson sounds similar to the word "dancing". The question is, how do we link the action of dancing with the person's face? If we look at the lips they appear very straight and to run almost right across the face. The eyebrows run parallel in a fashion across the top of the face. With a little imagination we can imagine these two features as a proscenium to a stage. Given that, let's picture the nose as a dancing ballerina.

To link the first name with the surname let's imagine we are looking through the mesh of a tennis racquet at the ballerina on stage.

Susan Price

The first name Susan can be represented by an image of a saucepan as they have near similar sounds. If we look at the lower half of the face and draw across the cheeks and round the chin we can imagine the bowl-shape of a saucepan. To add to this mnemonic, think of the tip of the nose as being the end of the handle of the saucepan. To help grasp this image, imagine holding a saucepan by the bowl and holding the tip of the handle close to you.

When creating mnemonics we must be prepared to look and handle things in different perspectives. I state again that making an extra effort and taking unusual steps pays dividends.

To create a mnemonic for the surname let's use a joke: "Did you hear about the man who bought a non-stick pan but couldn't get the label off?" To create a mnemonic for the surname Price think of the lips and mouth area as being a price label, stuck on the side of the pan.

Oliver Pierceson

It might be too easy to think as this person's eyes as two black olives to give us a mnemonic for the first name Oliver. For the surname Pierceson, we could think of him as having piercing eyes. But I suspect that we might be able to recall the first name but struggle to recall the surname at a later date. We might realise that the mnemonic has something to do with the eyes but the word piercing may not spring to mind quite so easily.

In such a case it is worthwhile making an extra effort. Given that we are using an image of olives for the first name and the word "piercing" for the surname, let's think about how we can link the two together. The answer is a cocktail stick. Olives are often seen pierced on a cocktail stick and we can make use of this fact.

The other prominent feature of this person's face is his long straight nose. Let's pierce a cocktail stick horizontally through his nose and then pierce an olive on each end.

Grace Williams

The first name Grace sounds similar to grass. The eyes appear to be quite small in comparison with the largeness of the face. If we were to imagine tufts of grass growing from the area around the eyes, then we should have a suitable mnemonic for the first name.

For the surname Williams, we can think of William Tell who was a famous Swiss folk hero who fired a crossbow. If we were to draw a line around the hairline, eyebrows and nose we can see a shape that will represent a crossbow.

Although I prefer not to use hairlines or feature that may change, I feel that this person's hair naturally grows away from the face and the crossbow pattern is unlikely to change.

To link the first name and surname together just imagine a crossbow lying in grass.

Sensational Memory

Random faces 21 to 30. Recall the correct name for each face.

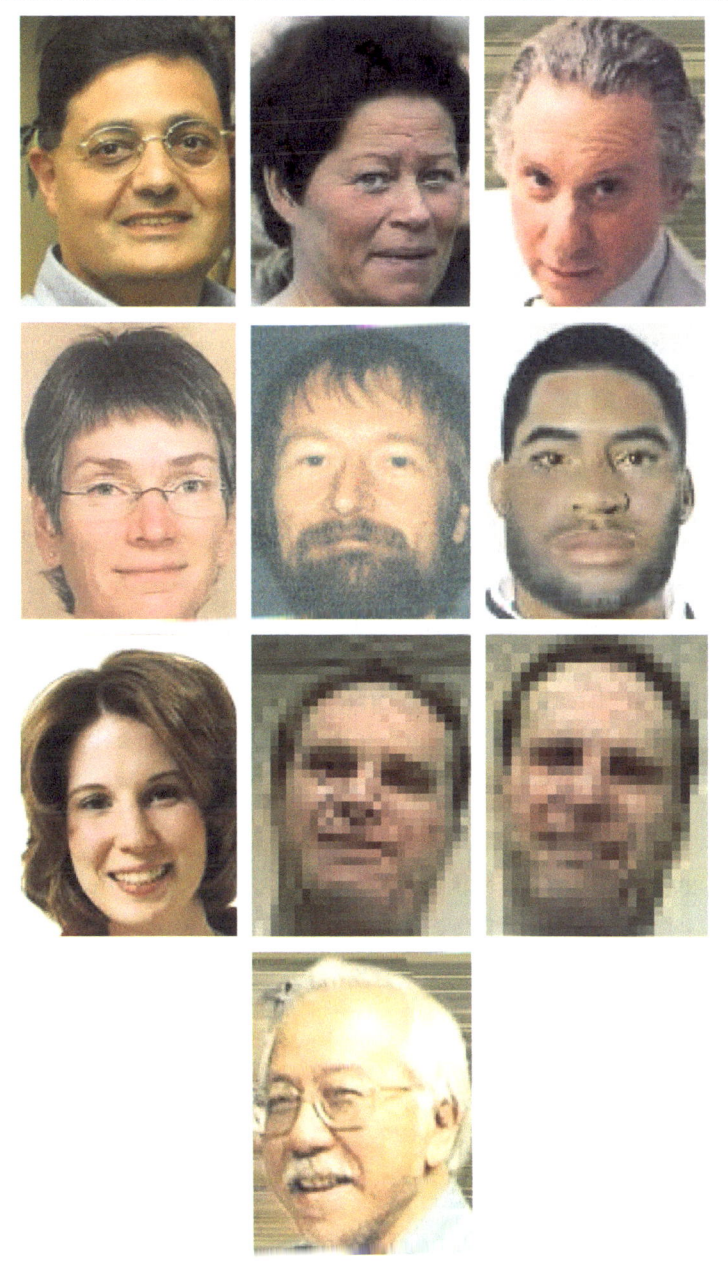

Faces 31 to 40

Larry Hawkins

Here again we are presented with identifying identical twins. A hat can represent the first name Larry from the association with the well-known song title *Hats off to Larry*. We need to think carefully where we are going to place a hat to formulate the mnemonic effectively. With a closer inspection of this person it appears that the eyebrows seem to lie heavier over his eyes than do his twin brother's. Let's make use of this slight difference and imagine that the eyebrows are the brim of a hat pushing down over the eyes.

The surname Hawkins can be represented simply by an image of a hawk. As we have already drawn attention to the eyebrows, there is no harm in perching a hawk with one talon on each eyebrow.

Malcolm Hawkins

To create a mnemonic for the name Malcolm may seem difficult at first. However, we can make use of the word "milk", which has similar sounding consonants to the first syllable of the first name.

This person's pupils appear marginally darker and more rounded than his twin brother's. If we imagine tears of milk falling from the eyes this should give us a powerful enough mnemonic for the first name.

If we imagine a hawk perched on his nose pecking at the teardrops of milk this should create a strong enough mnemonic for the first name and the surname combined.

Julie Adams

The first name Julie sounds similar to jewellery. If you are to use an image of jewellery it is best to picture a piece of jewellery that you own or that is familiar to you. The area around this person's eyes is very dark. A piece of shiny gold or silver jewellery would stand out against such a dark background.

The surname Adams can be represented by an image of an apple because we can think of Adam's apple. As this person's eyes are deep set it makes her cheeks more prominent. We can picture the rounded cheekbones as being apples.

To link the first name and surname together imagine the stalks of the apples hanging from the piece of jewellery around the eyes.

Nigel Attwell

The first name may present us with some difficulty in creating a mnemonic. However, with a little imagination and licence such difficulty is not insurmountable. If we look at the first syllable of the first name we will notice that it sounds the same as the first syllable of the word knight. As this person is male we can make some association with a knight, which is a male figure.

The lines and features of this face are quite well defined and appear symmetrical. If we imagine this face to be the helmet of a suit of armour with a visor etc. then we should have an effective mnemonic for the first name. The eyes are quite narrow and we could imagine him peering through the visor of the helmet.

If we wish, we could imagine some sort of gel coming from his mouth to give us a mnemonic for the second syllable.

A hat can represent the first syllable of the surname. A well can represent the second syllable.

To link the two names together, imagine a knight charging along on horseback, with a lance that has a hat balanced on the end. See the knight drop the hat into a well.

Jack Perkins

A British Union Jack flag can represent the first name Jack. This person's nose is very straight and we could think of it as a flagpole to which the Union Jack is attached.

A coffee percolator could represent the surname Perkins as the word and the name share a similar sounding first syllable. This person's forehead is rectangular in shape and we could imagine it being a container for coffee and further imagine the coffee percolating downwards between the eyebrows and into the nose.

Two link the first name to the surname imagine coffee trickling or percolating down the flagpole.

Jennifer Francis

The first name Jennifer can be represented by an image of jellyfish as they share a similar sound. The eyes of this person's face are very noticeable and if we were to substitute them with jellyfish we would have a suitable mnemonic for the first name.

For the surname we can use a famous figure that shares the same name. In this instance, we could think of Sir Francis Drake. We can use an image of a drake (male duck) to animate our mnemonic.

This person's nose appears to be quite long and straight. Let's imagine a drake walking sideways with its webbed feet up and down the length of the nose. In fact, just an image of webbed feet walking along sideways will be sufficient to give us the surname.

To link both names we can imagine a drake pecking into the jellyfish.

Mandy Jenkins

For this person's first name I am going to draw on a corny joke that I learned as a young child. Remember that some of the best mnemonics are created when new information is attached to long established information. Sometimes the old established information may be quite unusual and might not be of much practical use to us, but for some reason we have carried this old anomalous information for years.

I am sure everybody has these unusual outcrops of old information and for most people they have no real value. However, for a mnemonist they are like a seam of gold.

When I first heard the joke I didn't find it particularly funny (still don't), nevertheless it has stuck in my mind and I can make use of it, for a purpose for which I'm sure it was not intended. Here is the long awaited joke:

Knock! Knock!

Who's there?

Mandy

Mandy who?

Mandy lifeboats we're sinking.

Given this, the name Mandy can be represented by an image of a lifeboat! Quite often when the sound of a name triggers an image we can find some feature of the person's face that we can associate with the image.

If we draw a line across the eyebrows and across the tops of the cheekbones, we can imagine the shape of a lifeboat.

It appears that one of this person's eyes is higher than the other. This in turn makes our boat appear as if one end is higher than the other. We can imagine the lifeboat being tossed amongst the waves. Imagine the eyes like small brown marbles rolling up and down the hull of the boat.

The surname Jenkins may require a leap of imagination to create a mnemonic. However, since our imaginations are virtually limitless it should not present too much of a problem.

The fist syllable of the surname sounds like the first syllable of general. The second syllable sounds like the word "king". A military general could be thought of as wearing a peak cap as part of his uniform. A king could be seen to be wearing a crown. In this instance, we can create some headwear that consists of half a peaked cap on one side and half of a crown on the other.

The peak cap should appear on our left and the crown on the right. This is so we can recall the syllables in the correct order from left to right.

As we have used a leap of imagination to create a mnemonic it is very important that we strategically place the headwear so that it interacts with the person's face. If we place the imaginary headwear at a tilted angle as if it is pushing the lower eye down then we will have a powerful mnemonic.

To link the first name and surname together we can imagine a general and a king on a lifeboat on a rough sea.

Vera Wilson

For the first name we can think of a weathervane or weathercock. This is because a weathervane is an implement that indicates how the wind may "veer". The question now is how do we attach a weathercock to this person's face?

This person's nose is quite long and straight and we could imagine this to be the stand on which the body of the weathercock would pivot. The body of the weathercock can be made from drawing a line around the hairline and the eyebrows. Imagine that the gap between the eyebrows would make the underbelly that would pivot on top of the nose.

Look at this person's picture and blow air on it and imagine the part of the face which forms the body of the weathercock spinning round. Taking physical action whilst using imagination is a powerful memory technique.

For the surname we can use the same features but imagine them forming a willow tree. The willow will give us the first syllable of the surname. For the second syllable we picture the sun shining through the willow tree branches.

To link the first name and the second name we can keep to a weather theme and think of the famous book *The Wind in the Willows*.

Gerry Harrison

The first name can be represented by a jerrycan. As the face appears to have an oblong shape, let's imagine that this person's face as an aerial view of a jerrycan. The nose is long and is quite a prominent feature and we could imagine the nose to be the handle of the jerrycan. However, the tip of the nose is quite bulbous and we could imagine it as being the screw cap of the can.

We can think of the word "hairy", as it sounds similar to the first two syllables of the surname. The eyes are another prominent feature and if we were to imagine lots of hair growing quickly from the eyes into the mouth we could create a powerful mnemonic.

The mouth is another prominent feature and if we were to think of the mouth as being a sun we would have a mnemonic for the last syllable. Especially if we were to think of the mouth swallowing the hair.

I am usually reluctant to use teeth for face and name recognition as the lips often cover them, teeth can be broken or dentures can be removed. However, in this instance I suspect that the teeth are frequently exposed and should not cause too much of a problem.

To link the surname to the first name imagine taking off the screw cap of the jerrycan (bulbous tip of the nose) and imagine hair growing out of it and being swallowed by the mouth.

Stephen Humphries

A steel fence can represent the first name, as the syllables of the first name match the first syllables of each of the words "steel fence". This person's chin appears to be quite square so it would be a good place to attach the steel fence.

A camel can represent the surname, as a camel has a hump. The word "hump" gives us the first syllable. The person's nose is the feature which most resembles a camel's hump. If we were to imagine a camel's hump covered with ice, this will give us the second syllable, as we can make an association with ice and the word freeze.

To link the first name with the surname focus on the lower portion of the face and picture a frozen camel's hump behind a steel fence. To add movement to the mnemonic, imagine the camel walking up and down the length of the fence.

Chris Hare

Random faces 31 to 40. Recall the correct name for each face.

Faces 41 to 52

Bob Lewis

This person would quite easily be noticeable in a crowd. The long hair, large spectacles and the beard make him appear rather distinct. However, as already stated, such features are easily changed or removed and could easily give a totally different appearance. Therefore we need to focus on features that are unlikely to change.

Let's deal with the first name Bob. Again I am going to draw upon an old joke to create a mnemonic:

What does a goldfish call his friend?

Answer: Bob

As this joke is more visual than verbal I will try to explain. When goldfish are swimming in the water the movement of their mouths appears as if they are miming the name Bob. Consequently we can now make an association with the name Bob and a goldfish.

This person's nose appears very long and straight but let's imagine his nose as a goldfish wiggling.

We have already dealt with somebody with the surname Lewis. It is not uncommon in a room full of people to have more than one person with the same surname, even though they may not be related. In such circumstances we need to create a different mnemonic and attach it to the first name.

If we look at this person's lips they are unusually very straight and also quite rich in colour. The rich colour of his lips may appear enhanced against the background of his fair skin.

Again we can use the image of a loo roll and snake to represent the name Lewis as discussed with a previous person. However, you may recall that we attached the loo roll and snake to the person's eyebrows. As in this instance we are using the lower part of this person's face, this will be enough to distinguish two people who share the same surname.

As we are dealing with somebody who has a shared surname, it is perhaps even more important that we make a strong link with the first name and surname.

Let's imagine the tail of the goldfish is brushing against the person's lips and as it does so the loo roll is dispensed from between the lips. Imagining contact and movement helps create a powerful mnemonic.

Paul Haynes

The first name can be represented by a mnemonic image of a ball. The letters b and p are similar in sound and are pronounced by using similar facial muscles. We could also think of an image of a wall, which rhymes with the first name.

This person has a very broad and prominent forehead. If we imagine his forehead as a wall with a ball bouncing against it we will have a suitable mnemonic for the first name.

For the surname we are going to look at the lower part of the face around the chin area. Again this area is prominent and the chin appears square, even if we were to ignore the beard.

In this area let's imagine there is a nest made from hay. However, the nest and hay give the syllables of the surname in reverse order. So to counteract this let's picture the nest as being placed upside down.

To link the first name and the surname let's imagine that a ball bounces against a wall which causes it to collapse on top of the nest, which is made of hay.

Philip Evans

For the first name we can think of the words "fill up". If we look at the overall shape of the person's face we can see that because of the broadness of the forehead and the narrowness of the chin, it almost takes the shape of a wine glass. As a wine glass is something that we might fill up, an image of a wine glass in this case will make a suitable mnemonic for the first name.

Again we have another repeated surname. You may recall the mnemonic image for the surname Evans as being a series of stars. In this instance we can attach the first name and surname together instantly. If we think of sparkling wine in the glass and the bubbles as being stars we will have a suitable mnemonic for both the first name and surname.

June Steadman

For the first name we can think of a musical instrument. This is because musical instruments are used for playing a tune which sounds similar to the first name. In this instance, let's think of the person's nose as a piccolo. Now let's think about a couple of other associations we can use to cement this mnemonic. This person's nose is quite short and a piccolo is a short wind instrument (compared with e.g. a flute).

We can also think of a person picking their nose, as the word pick is the first syllable of the word piccolo.

For the surname we are going to have to grant ourselves some considerable licence and use our imagination. There are two vertical lines, one each side of the corners of the mouth. These together with the mouth could appear as a four-poster bed. Here we can make an association with the word bedstead.

With a little further imagination we could picture a dead man in the bed. In fact, we can think of the person's teeth as being a skeleton. These associations should be enough to give us a strong enough mnemonic for the surname.

To link the first name and surname, imagine the piccolo puncturing through the roof of the four-poster bed and playing a tune almost loud enough to wake the dead.

Irene Johnson

For this person's first name we can think of an eye, as this word has the same sound as the first syllable. For the second syllable there is no ideal similar sounding word. However, we can think of rain, as the r and n sound are similar and fall in the same order.

Fortunately, we can make an association with these two words. We can think of eyes having tears of rain. This person's eyes may not the most prominent feature on her face, but they are the darkest points given her very fair complexion. So if we picture tears of rain falling from this person's eyes we should have a suitable mnemonic for her first name.

We use the image of a toilet to represent the name John - John is an American slang word for toilet. If we picture this person peering through a toilet seat we will have a mnemonic for the first syllable of the surname. If we picture a dark or black toilet seat this will give us a contrast to her fair skin. For the second syllable we can picture her face as a shining sun.

Although the image of her face as a sun may be considered a weak mnemonic we can look at some of the other images and find that there is a connecting theme. That is to say the words "rain, fair and sun" are all words that come under the "umbrella" of the weather.

Although in this instance, an umbrella is not a mnemonic image that we use to remember this particular face, it is useful to create puns or jokes that cause a mental reaction thereby strengthening the mnemonic.

Keith Norris

For the first name we can think of a key. The jagged edges on the stem of a key are known as teeth. Fortunately, the word teeth rhymes with the first name and therefore suits our purpose.

For the first syllable of the surname we can think of a mouse as a mouse gnaws things. Gnawing is a very destructive action and makes a powerful mnemonic.

Chris Hare

For the second syllable we can think of rice. Although this is not an ideal sounding word, we can associate it with the word gnaw, as it is edible.

In this instance I am going to combine the ideas of the first name and surname to create one moving image. Having thought of key and mouse we can now think of a toy clockwork mouse. To make sure that we get the first name, we need to see a large key being inserted into the mouse. We should also see the key turning as the mouse scurries mechanically.

The shape of the lower part of the face below the nose and around the chin resembles the shape and size of a rice bowl. Let's picture the clockwork mouse gnawing the rice in the bowl. To help us draw attention to this image, imagine the eyes of the person looking down into the rice bowl and observing the activity.

Ken Young

In this instance we can combine the first name and the surname. We can think of a Kenyan simply because it sounds very similar to both names. However, we still need to create a mnemonic that we can attach to the person's face, as a play on words is not usually powerful enough on its own.

So let's look at some things that are associated with a Kenyan. A Kenyan comes Kenya, which is renowned for its safaris. If we look at the area of this person's head above his eyebrows, it is very pale in complexion. This is in contrast to the dark area around his eyes. Furthermore, the shape of his head above the eyebrows resembles that of a pith helmet.

Given the pale complexion and the shape of the area mentioned, we can imagine this person to be wearing a white or light coloured pith helmet. We can further imagine that the areas around the eyes are very dark as they are a shadow created by the pith helmet.

Imogen Scott

For the first name we need only create a mnemonic for the first syllable. We could think of a mirror and think of "mirror image". The word "image" will give us the first syllable. This person's face appears quite flat as the cheeks are not particularly rounded and the sides of the face are quite long. Let's imagine that this flat appearance is because she is pushing her face onto the surface of a mirror.

The oval shape of her face also resembles a large hand mirror (the type of mirror that is not dissimilar to the shape of a table tennis bat).

As there is not likely to be another name that begins with the sound of the word "image", there is no need to create a mnemonic for the second syllable.

For the surname we can think of Scott of the Antarctic. Let's imagine the shape of the face as an entrance to an igloo. Let's further imagine that the flatness of the face was caused by the strong Antarctic winds.

It is worth bearing in mind that when we see a certain distinguishing feature or facial shape, that we may employ that characteristic for more than one name. When you recognise such a feature and you are able to recall one of the names it is worth asking yourself if that feature might resemble something else or have been used to create yet another mnemonic for another name.

In this instance, we can combine the two names by thinking of an igloo with a mirrored door.

Michael O'Keefe

For the first name Michael we can think of the fish mackerel as this word has a similar sound to the first name. In this instance the person's ears have a similar shape to that of fish. So if we think of these ears as mackerel, we will have a suitable mnemonic for the first name.

It is not usually advisable to use ears for mnemonics as different hairstyles or a hat can easily cover them. However, in this instance the hairstyle is unlikely to change and the ears appear to be set quite low down on the side of the head and are unlikely to be covered.

For the surname we can think of an orange to represent the first syllable of the name simply because an orange is a bright colourful fruit that begins with the letter O.

For the second syllable again we can think of an image of a key. We can combine the two syllables with one mnemonic by thinking of the book and film title *Clockwork Orange*.

Now let's create a mnemonic image for both the first name and surname. Imagine a key being inserted through an orange and into a mackerel (ears).

We can further strengthen this image by turning the key causing the orange and mackerel to rotate. There is also another association we can make by thinking about a tin of fish which usually has a key attached.

Henry Thomas

Again, for the first name Henry we need to create a mnemonic for the first syllable only. This is quite simply to picture a hen. If we look at this person's eyes they appear very narrow. Let's imagine that they are being pushed downwards because there is a hen nesting on them.

For the surname we can think of tomatoes as they have a similar sound to Thomas. In this instance we can think of squashed tomatoes.

Let's combine these two names by picturing the hen squashing the tomatoes as it rests above the eyes. As we have discussed that the eyes are narrow because they are being pushed down, we already have a sensation of squashing.

To make the mnemonic stronger, imagine the juice of the tomatoes being absorbed by the feathers of the hen and also see the pips and juice trickling into the person's eyes causing him to squint.

Graham Murphy

For the first name we can think of a greyhound. This person has quite a long and thin face and we can easily make some association with the face of a greyhound.

For the surname we can think of the word "mirth". However, we need something to represent an image of mirth. In this instance we are going to have to search a little wider to find a representative image.

The word "mirth" conjures up an image of laughter. If we think of the famous painting called *The Laughing Cavalier* we could place a cavalier's hat on the head of a greyhound. This person's eyes appear quite narrow and we could think of them being under the cavalier's hat.

Peter Askew

This person's first name can be represented by the image of a pizza and as he has got a large round face it is quite easy to make an association.

For the surname we can think of a skewer and combine both the names by imagining a pizza being impaled and spinning on a skewer. Furthermore, see the pizza tilted at an angle and think of it being askew.

Sensational Memory

Random faces 41 to 52. Recall the correct name for each face.

- 227 -

Chris Hare

Recall the correct name for all 52 faces placed in the order below:

Sensational Memory

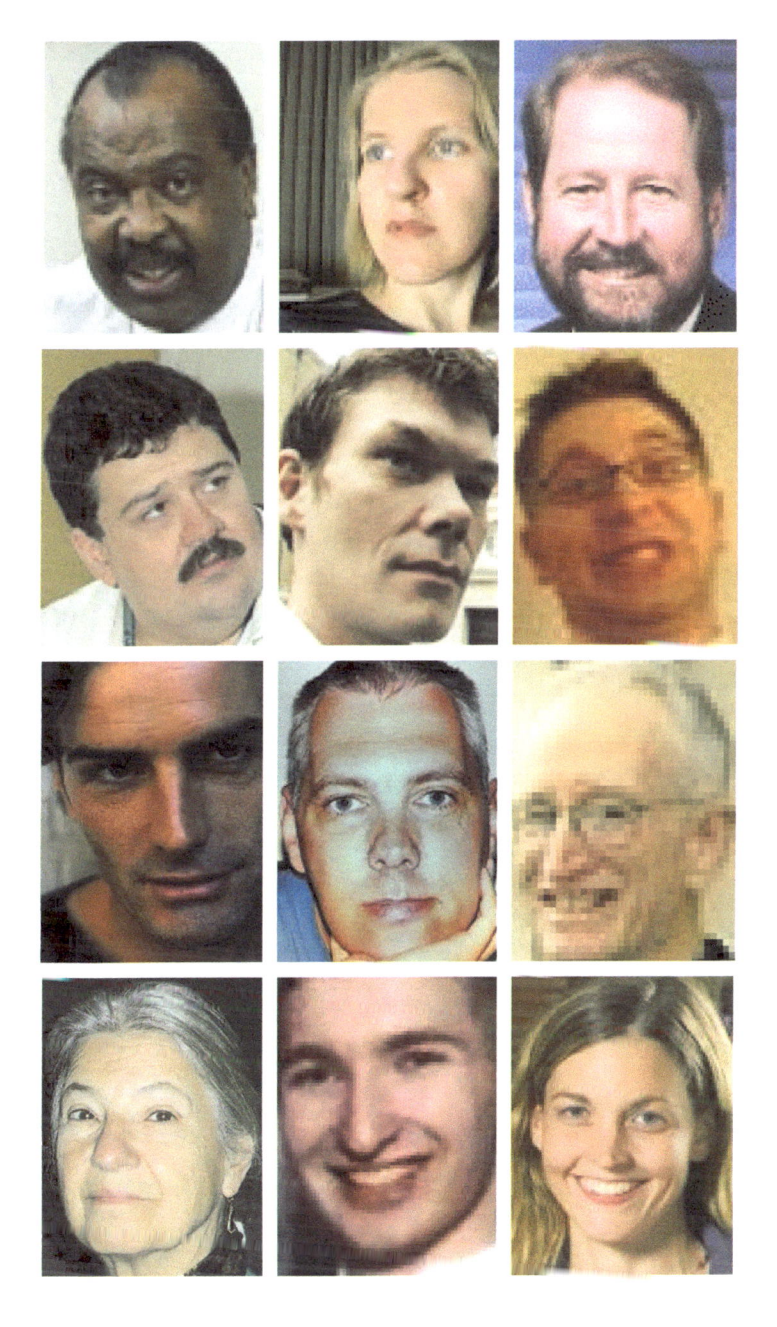

Chris Hare

Sensational Memory

Chris Hare

Chapter 18

Memorising A Deck of Cards

The feat of memorising a deck of cards is a worthwhile skill to acquire as it helps enhance and maintain the mind's sharpness, creativity and capability. Also, a deck of cards is something that is an inexpensive item to carry on your person and can be easily employed when you have a few minutes to spare. Simply by shuffling and changing the order of the deck creates an interesting and different challenge virtually every time, as there are 2,704 possible permutations (excluding jokers).

The first thing that we need to do is establish a Mnemonic Journey of 52 different locations. We have already discussed in chapter 14 about creating a Mnemonic Journey. You may, if you wish, use the first 52 places of your Mnemonic Journey that you have already learned, or create a new journey of 52 places for this exercise. I would suggest at this initial stage that you use the journey that you have already learned as this will help you reinforce your images of that journey. These 52 locations will represent the position of each card in the deck.

Having established how these 52 positions may appear in a Mnemonic Journey we will need to create a further 52 mnemonic images to represent each card. The mnemonic images of the cards are created in a not too dissimilar fashion from when we first learnt the Mnemonic Alphabet. In fact, we will use the Mnemonic Alphabet to represent the face value of each of the cards from ace (1) to 10. Therefore, if you have a full understanding of the Mnemonic Alphabet then you will already have a good foundation for being able to perform this particular feat. We will, of course, deal with the court cards (Jack, Queen, King) in due course.

The suits are simply represented by their initial letter (C - Clubs, H - Hearts, S - Spades and D - Diamonds). This simple system accompanied with the Mnemonic Alphabet will give us opportunities to create words to make visual images. However, the representative letters may appear in reverse order (i.e. the suit may occasionally appear before the numerical value of the card). With a little practice this will not prove a problem at all.

Let's begin to create a mnemonic image for each card in order of the four suits: Clubs, Hearts, Spades and Diamonds (known as "CHaSeD" order).

CLUBS

Ace of Clubs

This card can be represented by the image of a black cat or any other colour cat, but as the Ace of Clubs is a black card it may be useful to think of a black cat. Let's look more closely as to why we would use the image of a cat. In this instance, the letter C represents the suit of Clubs simply because the suit begins with the letter C.

Sensational Memory

The ace has a numerical value of one. In the Mnemonic Alphabet the letter T represents the number one. By simply placing the vowel "a" between the C and T we can create the word cat to give us a suitable mnemonic image.

Two of Clubs

This card can be represented by the image of a giraffe. In the Mnemonic Alphabet the letter N represents the number two. Again the letter C represents the suit of Clubs. Using these mnemonic letters we can create the word neck and as a giraffe is renowned for having a very long neck we can use an image of this animal to represent the Two of Clubs.

Three of Clubs

To represent this card we use the image of a microphone (commonly abbreviated to mic - pronounced mike). The letter M represents the number three in the Mnemonic Alphabet and again the letter C represents the suit of Clubs.

Four of Clubs

An image of a rake can be representative of the Four of Clubs. The number four is represented by the mnemonic letter R. However, we will allow ourselves a little licence by using the letter K which a hard C sound to represent the suit of Clubs. This ploy of substituting similar sounding letters will prove to be very useful.

Five of Clubs

The Five of Clubs can be represented by a mnemonic image of a lock or a key. A giant padlock would suit our purpose. We form the image of a lock because the letter L in the Mnemonic

Alphabet represents the number five and the hard C sound represents the suit of Clubs.

Six of Clubs

The Six of Clubs can be represented by an image of a sack as the letter S represents the number six and the hard C sound represents the suit of Clubs.

Seven of Clubs

The Seven of Clubs can be represented by the mnemonic image of a cake (if you wish you could imagine a birthday cake with seven burning candles).

Eight Of Clubs

The Eight of Clubs can be represented by a jar of coffee as the letter C represents the suit of Clubs and the letter F in the Mnemonic Alphabet represents the number eight.

Nine of Clubs

A cup can represent the Nine of Clubs. The letter C represents the suit of Clubs and the letter P from the Mnemonic Alphabet represents the number nine.

Ten of Clubs

Creating a mnemonic for the Ten of Clubs may present a few problems. However, we could use an image of a cosy or tea cosy. The word cosy as a noun is defined as a cover to keep something warm. In the case of a tea cosy it is a covering which is placed over a teapot (there are thousands of images of these on the Internet).

The letter C will represent the suit of Clubs. However, we may grant ourselves some licence with the letter S as in this instance the letter S is pronounced as a Z. In fact, the American spelling is tea cozy.

Jack of Clubs

A cage can represent the Jack of Clubs. The letter C represents the suit of Clubs. Again, we are going to grant ourselves some licence. The latter part of the word cage is similar to that of the phonetic sound of the letter J.

Queen of Clubs

A duck can represent the Queen of Clubs. This is because the sound made by a duck is "quack". In this instance the Q represents the Queen and the C sounds represents the suit of Clubs.

King of Clubs

The King of Clubs can be represented by a cook. It may be easier for us to picture a chef wearing a tall hat. The letter C represents the suit of Clubs and the letter K represents the face value of a King.

Exercise

Familiarise yourself with the 13 mnemonic images that you have just learnt for the suit of Clubs. From your deck of playing cards, remove the suit of Clubs and shuffle them and use your mnemonic skills to memorise and recall the cards in their new order.

It is possible to memorise an entire deck of cards without using a location or journey system. We could use a link system whereby we have the mnemonic images of the cards interact with each other. For example, a cat padlocked to the handle of a cup and within that cup rests a microphone would represent the order of Ace of Clubs, Five of Club, Nine of Clubs and Three of Clubs.

However, this may not necessarily enable you to recall a card at any randomly named position. For example, if somebody was to ask you what card is in the 16th position in the deck, you may not be able to recall that card without recalling the previous cards in order. Using a location/journey system will facilitate this task quite simply once you have mastered the technique.

With a little practice it is no more time consuming to memorise and recall a deck of cards by combining a link system with a location/journey system.

In Chapter 13 I gave an example of the beginnings of a location/journey system. You may recall that you should create your own personal system by using locations that are familiar to you. In this instance, each location will represent a position in a deck of cards. To memorise a deck of cards (excluding jokers) you will, of course, need to memorise and familiarise yourself with 52 locations in a strictly set order.

1. Front garden wall

2. Gate

3. Bird table

4. Fishpond

5. Garage

6. Clothesline

7. Statue

8. Fireplace

9. Stairs

10. Bathroom

Let's use the above example location/journey list to memorise the first 10 cards from the suit of Clubs. You may prefer to use a location system that you have already learnt. As it is not possible for me to know what personal locations you are using, I will demonstrate by using the 10 locations above.

The following is a random order of 10 playing cards:

7C, QC, 3C, 6C, 8C, 5C, 10C, AC, JC, KC

1. The Seven of Clubs is represented by a cake. The first location (in my system) is a front garden wall. I simply picture a cake with its burning candles resting on that specific wall. I also imagine a few crumbs of cake falling on to the wall.

2. The image for the Queen of Clubs is a duck (quack) and the second location is a gate. Here I picture a duck standing on the gate. I also zoom in and see the webbed feet making contact with the gate. As webbed feet inherently belong to a duck and there is no other similar mnemonic image, simply seeing and feeling that contact is sufficient to give me a suitable mnemonic.

3. The image for the Three of Clubs is a microphone, which we can place in the third location which is a bird table.

4. The Six of Clubs is represented as a sack, which we can picture being dropped into a fishpond. However, I may just see this image as a plastic bag containing a goldfish as traditionally seen at a funfair. Taking this extra leap of imagination and combining associations (in this case a fish and a sack) makes a very powerful mnemonic. With a little practice, you will begin to create these combinations for yourself. In fact, they develop subconsciously and present themselves naturally.

5. The mnemonic image for the Eight of Clubs is a jar of coffee. Simply see a giant coffee jar placed in front of a garage. We could take this a step further and imagine that the garage doors are unable to close due to being blocked by the giant coffee jar.

6. The Five of Clubs is represented by a mnemonic image of a lock (padlock) that we can easily imagine being securely fastened onto a clothesline, which represents the sixth position.

7. The mnemonic image for the Ten of Clubs is a cosy or tea cosy. The seventh position is represented by a mnemonic image of a statue. If we assume that the statue features a human face, we can place the tea cosy over the face. Imagine the nose protruding through the hole in the tea cosy where the spout of a teapot would normally fit.

It is advisable to make use of this feature of the tea cosy whenever possible in creating a mnemonic for the Ten of Clubs. Making use of such features for different purposes (e.g. substituting the spout for a nose) is a powerful technique.

8. The mnemonic image for the Ace of Clubs is that of a black cat. The eighth position is represented by the image of a fireplace. Given these two images we have plenty of scope for implementing many of the techniques we have learnt for

creating powerful mnemonic images (e.g. movement, pain, sound and humour etc.).

Let's imagine that a black cat has fallen down a chimney and rolled out of the fireplace and onto the hearth. It is worth making note that the name "Sooty" is a popular name for a pet black cat. This name can easily be associated with a fireplace and black cat.

9. The Jack of Clubs is represented by a cage. An image of a birdcage would be suitable as its size is more versatile than a lion's cage or bear cage etc. In this instance we can imagine a birdcage rattling as it tumbles down a staircase. I would, however, advise that we avoid an image of a bird as it may distract from, or overshadow what we are essentially trying to recall.

10. The King of Clubs is represented by a cook (chef) and we could imagine him preparing food in a bathroom. For example, we can imagine him peeling vegetables and depositing the vegetable skin in the sink, bath and toilet.

For the remaining cards in the suit (2C, 4C and 9C), attach them to whatever mnemonic locations you may have for positions 11, 12 and 13.

To complete the exercise, recall the order of the cards by using the mnemonic images that you have created.

HEARTS

The letter H will feature in the construction of the mnemonic words/images for each of the cards in the suit of Hearts.

Let's create mnemonic images for each of the thirteen cards:

Ace of Hearts

The mnemonic image for the Ace of Hearts is constructed from the letter H and the letter T to form the word and image of a hat (remember that T is the mnemonic letter for the number 1 which represents an Ace in a deck of playing cards).

Two of Hearts

The mnemonic image for the Two of Hearts is constructed from the letter H and the letter N to form the word and image of a hen.

Three of Hearts

The mnemonic image for the Three of Hearts is constructed from the letter H and the letter M to form the word and image of ham. In this instance we could picture a slice of ham as pink meat. However, I prefer to use an image of a pig as ham is produced from the meat of a pig and we can easily make an association between these two things. An image of a pig is far more versatile for the purpose of mnemonics than a slice of meat.

Four of Hearts

The mnemonic image for the Four of Hearts is constructed from the letter H and the letter R to form the word and image of a hare. Although it is advisable to use the sound of a rolling R when creating a mnemonic word that features the number four, I feel that an image of a hare is suitable to represent the Four of Hearts.

Five of Hearts

The mnemonic image for the Five of Hearts is constructed from the letter H and the letter L to form the word heel. In this instance we can think of an image of a high-heeled or stiletto-heeled shoe.

Six of Hearts

The mnemonic image for the Six of Hearts is constructed from the letter H and the letter S to form the word and image of a house. We can perhaps think of a doll's house as its size may be more suitable for placing in various locations.

Seven of Hearts

The mnemonic image for the Seven of Hearts is constructed from the letter H and the letter K to form the word and image of a hook.

Eight of Hearts

The mnemonic image for the Eight of Hearts is constructed from the letter H and the letter F to form the word and image of a hoof. However, I prefer to use an image of a horseshoe, which is easily associated with the image of a hoof.

Nine of Hearts

The mnemonic image for the Nine of Hearts is constructed from the letter H and the letter P to form the word and image of a hoop.

Ten of Hearts

The mnemonic image for the Ten of Hearts is constructed from the letter H and the sound of Z to represent the number ten.

Although it is spelt with an S we can think of the word hose as the S is pronounced as a Z. We can perhaps think of a garden hose, which is traditionally green in colour.

Jack of Hearts

The mnemonic image for the Jack of Hearts is constructed from the letter H and the J sound to form the word and image of a hedge.

Queen of Hearts

The mnemonic image for the Queen of Hearts is constructed from the letter H and the letter Q to form the word and image of the Greek god Hercules. The H represents the suit of Hearts and the Q sound in the second syllable of Hercules, represents the face value of a Queen.

King of Hearts

The mnemonic image for the King of Hearts is constructed from the letter H and the letter K to form the word and image of a hawk.

Exercise

Familiarise yourself with the mnemonic images for the suit of Hearts. Then take the cards for suit of Hearts and shuffle them into a random order. Memorise and recall all thirteen cards in their new order.

You will need to attach your new mnemonic images to your location/journey list from 14 through to 26. When you have created an image for the cards positioned 14 to 26, recall all the cards from both suits.

SPADES

The letter S will feature in the construction of the mnemonic words/images for each of the cards in the suit of Spades.

Let's create mnemonic images for each of the thirteen cards:

Ace of Spades

The mnemonic image for the Ace of Spades is constructed from the letter S and the letter T to form the word and image of a suit. The letter S represents the suit of Spades and the T represents the Ace (as previously discussed). It may help to think of a suit on a tailor's dummy or a mannequin. A pinstriped suit would make an ideal striking mnemonic image.

Two of Spades

The mnemonic image for the Two of Spades is constructed from the letter S and the letter N to form the word and image of a sun.

Three of Spades

The mnemonic image for the Three of Spades is constructed from the letter M and the letter S to form the word and image of a mouse.

Four of Spades

The mnemonic image for the Four of Spades is constructed from the letter R and the letter S to form the word and image of a rose.

Five of Spades

The mnemonic image for the Five of Spades is constructed from the letter S and the letter L to form the word and image of a sail (sailing boat/yacht).

Six of Spades

The mnemonic image for the Six of Spades is constructed by using the letter S twice to form a mnemonic image that represents the face value and suit of this particular card. Using these letters we can form the word and image of a sausage. In this instance we will grant ourselves a little licence by ignoring the last three letters of the word sausage. We can think of the sound of a sausage sizzling in a pan which makes a continuous S or hissing sound which we can use to associate the two mnemonic letters S and S.

The rules for mnemonics are not always hard and fast as demonstrated by the above example. This demonstration is given to open your mind to other possible alternatives when creating mnemonics.

Let's look at another example that keeps more or less within the rules of the Mnemonic Alphabet. It is evident that we need a double S sound for this particular card. We could think of the word sauce. We an easily picture brown sauce or tomato ketchup being spread over our location/journey mnemonic in any given position.

Seven of Spades

The mnemonic image for the Seven of Spades is constructed from the letter S and the letter K to form the word and image of a sock. However, we need to make a mental note not to confuse this image with the Six of Clubs, which has the same sounding mnemonic letters. To help us we can think of the shape of a sock as being a similar shape to an inverted number 7.

Eight of Spades

The mnemonic image for the Eight of Spades is constructed from the letter S and the letter F to form the word and image of a safe.

Nine of Spades

The mnemonic image for the Nine of Spades is constructed from the letter P and the letter S to form the word and image of peas.

Ten of Spades

The mnemonic image for the Ten of Spades would usually be constructed from the letter Z and the letter S to form an image of the Greek god Zeus. However, since we have already used an image of a Greek god (Queen of Hearts) this may cause confusion. So we could use an image of someone that we know called Suzi. We could perhaps think of the seventies rock star Suzi Quatro, whose first name is spelt Suzi. There are several images of Suzi Quatro to be found on the Internet. The iconic image of this '70s rock star was that of a petite, blonde-haired woman wearing a black leather suit and carrying a large electric guitar.

However, you may have enough knowledge of Greek mythology to have a defined image of different Greek gods and an image of Zeus may be most suitable for you.

Another possibility could be to think of a group of animals that are found in zoos. We can easily imagine this group of different animals charging through our location/journey mnemonic image.

Jack of Spades

The mnemonic image for the Jack of Spades is constructed from the letter J and the letter S to form the word and image of juice (the word juice ends with an S sound).

Queen of Spades

The mnemonic image for the Queen of Spades is constructed from the letter S and the letter Q to form the word and image of an Indian squaw. We could also reverse these mnemonic letters and think of the fictional hunchback character Quasimodo.

King of Spades

The mnemonic image for the King of Spades is constructed from the letter S and the letter K to form the word and image of a skier. Although an image of a single ski would adhere more closely to the rules of alphabetic mnemonics, there are far better possibilities for visualising a person skiing as an image of a skier enables us to imagine action.

Exercise

Familiarise yourself with the mnemonic images for the suit of Spades. Then take the suit of Spades and shuffle them into a random order. Memorise and recall all thirteen cards in their new order.

You will need to attach your new mnemonic images to your location/journey list from 27 through to 40. When you have created an image for the cards positioned 27 to 40, recall all the cards from the three suits in the order of Clubs, Hearts and Spades.

DIAMONDS

The letter D will feature in the construction of the mnemonic words/images for each of the cards in the suit of Diamonds.

Let's create mnemonic images for each of the thirteen cards:

Ace of Diamonds

The mnemonic image for the Ace of Diamonds is constructed from the letter T and the letter D to form the word and image of a toad.

Two of Diamonds

The mnemonic image for the Two of Diamonds is constructed from the letter D and the letter N to form the word and image of a Great Dane (breed of dog).

Three of Diamonds

The mnemonic image for the Three of Diamonds is constructed from the letter M and the letter D to form the word and image of a maid. In this instance we could perhaps picture a traditional serving maid in a black dress and a white pinafore.

Four of Diamonds

The mnemonic image for the Four of Diamonds is constructed from the letter R and the letter D to form the word and image of a rod (fishing). We could also think of the colour red to represent this card and paint our location/journey mnemonic red.

Five of Diamonds

The mnemonic image for the Five of Diamonds is constructed from the letter D and the letter L to form the word and image of a doll.

Six of Diamonds

The mnemonic image for the Six of Diamonds is constructed from the letter S and the letter D to form the word and image of a sod (of earth). It may help to picture a cutting of turf because a brown sod of earth is too bland a colour to make a naturally strong mnemonic.

Seven of Diamonds

The mnemonic image for the Seven of Diamonds is constructed from the letter K and the letter D to form the word and image of a kid (baby goat). You may prefer to picture a small child as children are often colloquially referred to as kids.

Eight of Diamonds

The mnemonic image for the Eight of Diamonds is constructed from the letter D and the letter F to form the word and image of a daff (informal name of a daffodil). Although the word daff is officially spelt with a double F, we are, of course, only concerned with a general F sound to represent the number eight.

This flower with its distinctive long green stem and brightly coloured head will make a powerful mnemonic image.

Nine of Diamonds

The mnemonic image for the Nine of Diamonds is constructed from the letter P and the letter D to form the word and image of a pad. In this instance we could perhaps picture a writing pad, notepad or any type of pad that springs to mind, so long as we are clear in our mind as to what this image represents.

Jack of Diamonds

The mnemonic image for the Jack of Diamonds is constructed from the letter J and the letter D to form the word and image of a Judo competitor. We can easily picture someone wearing traditional judo attire (e.g. a white tunic with a black belt).

Queen of Diamonds

The mnemonic image for the Queen of Diamonds is constructed from the letter Q and the letter D to form the word and image of a quad bike. There are several images of this type of vehicle which can be found on the Internet.

King of Diamonds

The mnemonic image for the King of Diamonds is constructed from the letter D and the letter K sound to form the word and image of a doc (doctor). Although in this instance the letter K does not feature in the mnemonic word, the hard C sound will represent the letter K for King card.

Exercise

Familiarise yourself with the mnemonic images for the suit of Diamonds. Then take the suit of Diamonds and shuffle them into a random order. Memorise and recall all thirteen cards in their new order.

You will need to attach your new mnemonic images to your location/journey list from 41 through to 52. When you have created an image for the cards positioned 41 to 52, recall all the cards from the four suits in the order of Clubs, Hearts and Spades and Diamonds.

Having familiarised yourself with all the images of the cards and completed the above exercise, shuffle the complete deck and memorise and recall the entire deck in any given random order.

Over the course of time you may find that your mnemonic images for some of the 52 cards will change to suit your preference. In fact, you may create images that do not necessarily follow the general rules of the Mnemonic Alphabet, so long as you have a strong mnemonic image for each of the 52 different cards that personally works for you.

With regular practice you will discover that you will be able to memorise and recall a complete deck of cards at a seemingly phenomenal speed.

Regularly practising of this exercise will keep your mind open to new and different possibilities with mnemonics. Creating mnemonics is an art form that can be continually adapted and improved.

This concludes *Sensational Memory* but I hope this is only a beginning for you, as the human mind is forever capable of pushing back its confines. Please practise the techniques and endeavour to develop techniques of your own.

Chris Hare September 2006